The Life of St. Francis of Assisi: A Compendium of the Early Legends

THE LIFE OF ST. FRANCIS OF ASSISI: A COMPENDIUM OF THE EARLY LEGENDS

Translated and Compiled by
Bret Thoman, OFS

TAN Books
Gastonia, North Carolina

Editrici Francescane, Via Orto Botanico, 11 - 35123 Padova
www.bibliotecafrancescana.it

Translated and Edited by Bret Thoman

Cover illustration: *Saint Francis of Assisi Receiving the Stigmata* (1767-1769) by Giovanni Battista Tiepolo. Public domain via Wikimedia Commons

Cover design by Caroline Green

ISBN: 978-1-5051-3587-9
Kindle ISBN: 978-1-5051-3589-3
ePUB ISBN: 978-1-5051-3588-6

Published in the United States by
TAN Books
PO Box 269
Gastonia, NC 28053
www.TANBooks.com

This book is dedicated to
all my Franciscan formators.

Contents

"The Rule and life of the Friars Minor is this: to observe the Holy Gospel of our Lord Jesus Christ by living in obedience, without anything of one's own, and in chastity."

—The Prologue of the Rule of St. Francis

Foreword

Bret Thoman's new book, *The Life of St. Francis of Assisi: A Compendium of the Early Legends*, is an interesting and important work. At first glance, it may appear to be a simple compilation of the events of the life of Saint Francis, extracted from the early biographies. But as any compilation, it reflects the spirituality of the author.

Thoman has a certificate in Franciscan spirituality and a master's degree in the Italian language. But he has also lived the Franciscan charism. For over two decades, Bret Thoman has been a professed member of the Secular Franciscan Order (formerly known as the Third Order of St. Francis). Moreover, he has spent many years visiting Franciscan sites throughout central Italy while accompanying groups and bringing pilgrims into the spirituality of the sites. Thus, the selection of excerpts and the crafting of the chronology of the events of the life of the Saint give insight into the spirituality and way of thinking of the author. How does he perceive the life of Saint Francis? What does he consider to be the most important moments of his life? How does he divide these moments? How does he begin? How does he conclude? Having lived the Franciscan vocation and walked in the footsteps of the saints, he has keen insight into the answers to these questions.

Thoman has already published very good books on Saint Francis and Clare and has also written on Franciscan spirituality. He has a deep knowledge of Franciscan spirituality and is familiar with the Italian language and culture. However, this latest book is a sort of experiment. He has endeavored to do what practically no one has ever done before. Bret has retranslated the early Franciscan legends, also known as the Sources, and pieced them together to create a new chronological life of Francis. The result is a great harmony among the works of the various early biographers.

While there are plenty of other biographies about Saint Francis in circulation, they usually reflect the life of Saint Francis through the filter of the writers' personal points of view, thus revealing the "colors" of the writers. But Bret has done something different. By returning to the early legends, Thoman has sought to present the life of Francis as it truly was historically. He has strived to represent St. Francis as he really was, stripped of the revisionism of many modern biographies of the saint. The result is something beautiful. It is as if he has gathered flowers from a meadow, given a special beauty to all of them, and made them into a bouquet.

This work is not a new biography of Saint Francis, but it is a new biography of Saint Francis. This book is not the work of Bret Thoman, but it is the work of Bret Thoman. All four statements are true. Ultimately, it doesn't matter. This work is a lovely collection of flowers, which together form a beautiful bouquet. I am sure that when you read this book, you will encounter this beauty.

—Tibor Kauser, OFS
Minister General of the Secular Franciscan Order

Preface

"Why after you, why after you, why is the whole world running after you?" Brother Masseo of Marignano posed this question to St. Francis, as narrated in *The Little Flowers* (chapter 10). Francis's response was that God chose a vile sinner such as him to confound the nobility and the wisdom of the world. He said that he had been chosen so that everyone would know that every virtue and every good come from God alone and not from any creature, and no person can boast in God's sight.

Whether or not this was the true reason the "whole world" was running after Francis in the thirteenth century is debatable. Ever humble, Francis could not have responded otherwise. He could not have referred to the natural gifts he had possessed since childhood—"cheerfulness, joyfulness, and gentleness," according to the early legends. Nor could he have taken credit for any of his spiritual charisms, as he fervently insisted that they were gifts from God and pointed to God and God alone.

Still today, people are running after St. Francis. The Poor Little One from Assisi continues to endear himself to the "whole world," including people of every religion and faith (or none at all). And just like Brother Masseo, contemporary people want to know what it is about him that makes him so attractive.

To this end, there is no shortage of research, studies, and books about St. Francis. It seems that new books on St. Francis are published every year. However, the biographies do not all say the same thing. While most claim to present the real St. Francis, the reality is that some modern accounts of the life of St. Francis are so divergent that they seem to have been written about different people.

Much of these discrepancies are due to the bias of the writers. It is said that a biography reveals more about the biographer than the subject. Biographers naturally focus on what interests them. How do they begin the story? What do they emphasize? What do they omit? How do they conclude?

Paul Sabatier (1858–1928) is considered the pioneer of modern Franciscan studies. He was the first historian to research the life of St. Francis by utilizing the historical-critical method. In 1894, he published the groundbreaking work, *Vie De S. François D'assise* (Life of St. Francis). A French Protestant in the Huguenot tradition, he winced at the "aureole and nimbus" and "hagiographical tinsel" he believed shrouded the authentic story of Francis of Assisi. He believed that the legends put forth by the saint's medieval biographers—which for centuries had framed the official narrative—were written more to bolster the Order's standing and strengthen the friars than to depict the true historical man from Assisi.

While Sabatier was a brilliant writer and systematic historian—and his descriptions of the spiritual life of St. Francis are truly stirring—his personal beliefs and assumptions as a Protestant minister in the Calvinist tradition heavily influenced his work, in particular, St. Francis's relationship to the Catholic Church and the hierarchy. Sabatier saw Francis as a prophetic reformer whose conversion was one of the heart and conscience, totally removed from the "hieratic clerics" of the canonical order.

Today, contemporary biographers continue to write about St. Francis, and many—in the footsteps of Sabatier—continue to do so through the filters of their spiritual or philosophical worldviews. Their biases have a say in the outcome of their work. In many of the contemporary biographies, Francis has become a standard bearer of one cause or another. Those who are more secular or not religious tend to emphasize the social aspects of St. Francis's life and how he transcended sectarian boundaries. These writers are often turned off by Francis's asceticism and are incredulous regarding miracles. Religious writers whose spirituality tends toward immanence (that is, Christ's dwelling in the world) also see Francis through the lens of social issues and his response to Jesus's requests to succor the Least Ones in Matthew 25. Their focus is on Francis's treatment of lepers and the poor, peacemaking efforts, and ecological concerns.

Another issue with the contemporary portraits of St. Francis is the development, nay, the evolution of Francis that has taken place over the years and decades. The more serious Franciscan biographers are well-versed in preceding biographies. But something that is merely suggested in one work becomes probable in the next. By the time it is quoted a third time, it is taken as fact. For example, in the footsteps of Sabatier, many contemporary writers accept as a fact that St. Francis was fiercely critical of the institutional Church and its wealth.

Elsewhere, other writers believe that St. Francis never received the stigmata. Chiara Frugone, an Italian medieval historian, in her 1993 work, *Francesco e l'invenzione delle stimmate* (Francis and the invention of the stigmata), expressed skepticism regarding the stigmata. While not entirely dismissing the miracle, she believed that the purported miracle was instrumentalized by the Franciscans to bolster the Order's reputation and further their religious and political agendas. By the time Donald Spoto wrote *Reluctant Saint* in 2002, Francis's alleged stigmata were "the scars of leprosy upon his body."

In other contemporary biographies, revealing the historical St. Francis is not even the objective. The spirit of St. Francis is the aim. St. Francis and his deeds have been reimagined for a modern audience. In the film world, Franco Zeffirelli's creative *Brother Sun, Sister Moon* (1972) epitomizes this reinvented Francis. A nature-loving, starry-eyed Francis wanders through fields in what comes across as a sentimental fairy tale more attuned to the countercultural ethos of the 1970s than the ascetic milieu of the early 1200s. It's as if

Francis has been revised to meet the demand of consumers hungry for a new and improved product.

St. Francis's encounter with the Islamic sultan of Egypt has also been reworked. The traditional account—that he went to the Muslim leader to preach Christ crucified, hoping he would convert and be baptized—has been brushed aside. Today, the event is seen as an original example of religious dialogue. Worse, it has led to St. Francis being seen as the model of religious pluralism.

Given so many contradictory—and false—portrayals of St. Francis, is there a way to arrive at the authentic St. Francis—the man the world was and is running after? Yes. The most authentic source of St. Francis is St. Francis himself. If someone truly wants to explore the original ideas, thoughts, values, and beliefs of St. Francis, he should read St. Francis's own writings. However, since St. Francis never wrote an autobiography, the next most authentic source of information about his life is the early biographies—that is, the thirteenth- and fourteenth-century legends. These works reveal the true St. Francis of Assisi. We do not have to explore the original legends in depth to see clearly that many of the contemporary perceptions of St. Francis are patently false.

The hierarchy: In the early legends, there is not one example of St. Francis appearing at odds with the Catholic hierarchy. On the contrary, he constantly appears exhorting his followers to respect priests—even if living in sin!—and to remain obedient to them as superiors. While he fully embraced poverty—in an era when, indeed, many clerics and prelates did not—Francis sought to convert through example, never through polemics.

Ecology: While St. Francis was declared the patron saint of ecologists in 1979 by Pope John Paul II, in many contemporary representations of the saint, his affinity for nature appears to flirt with pantheism. Yes, St. Francis perceived the created world around him fraternally—which is fully expressed in his beautiful prayer, *Canticle of Creatures*—but this is because he saw himself and all creation as created by the same Creator, God. Thus, his reverence for worldly creatures flowed from his worship of God; that is, he saw the goodness of creation as a reflection of the source: its origin in God.

The stigmata: Many contemporary skeptics have gone to great lengths to force a rational explanation regarding St. Francis and the stigmata. However, all the early legends heavily emphasize the event as miraculous.

Shortly after Francis's death, Brother Elias, the vicar, wrote a letter to all the friars, in which he intuited the event as evidence of Francis's particular conformity to Christ. Moreover, there were numerous eyewitnesses—including a pope—who described in detail and swore to what they saw.

The meeting with the sultan: In the early sources (including at least two non-Franciscan chroniclers who were eyewitnesses), the encounter between Francis and the sultan is described as an effort of evangelization. After receiving permission from the local ordinary of Akro (today Acre, northern Israel), Francis went to the sultan to preach salvation through the cross of Christ. He hoped he and Muslims everywhere would be baptized, which would lead to the end of the Crusades. If not, he was prepared to die a martyr. While there is some embellishment as the story progressed over the decades (the later sources claim the sultan secretly wished to be baptized and was done so in a vision on his deathbed, the early legends are of one mind in the depiction of the event. One may infer that the "dialogue" that took place between the two religious leaders led to the institution of the Custody of the Holy Land, which the Franciscan Order continues to administer to this day. However, Francis's intentions were clear.

Above are just some examples of how the historical St. Francis has been rejected in favor of the spirit of Francis. In the same way the late nineteenth- and early twentieth-century biographers sought to uncover the "real" Francis by stripping away the iconographic embellishment of a bygone era, I believe it is time to do the same today. Paradoxically, by returning to the ancient sources, we will see how many of the narratives that were developed in the twentieth and twenty-first centuries are false. And I also believe it is there that we will find the answer to the question, "Why after you?"

Editor's Note

To create this new compendium, I have selected various passages from the thirteenth- and fourteenth-century Franciscan legends, which I ordered chronologically to create a new narrative.

All the passages in this book were taken and translated from the Italian edition of the early Franciscan legends, known as the *Fonti Francescane* (Franciscan sources). The Italian volume—a translation, in turn, of the early sources from Latin—was initially published in 1977 but updated as recently as 2011.

The Italian *Fonti* utilizes a unique numbering system to reference each passage. In this work, I have cited the original source in the footnotes (e.g., the *Legend of the Three Companions*), followed by the corresponding Italian reference number. In this way, someone with access to the Italian edition (and Italian language skills) can look up the passage for more context. The

Fonti Francescane can be found online on a variety of websites.

Regarding language, there are some peculiarities used in the era of St. Francis. For example, the title or greeting, "lord," was used not only for the nobility but also for prelates of high office, such as cardinals and popes. A common form of address for men of lesser rank was Messer, which was used to show respect and politeness, especially towards individuals of higher social status, even in religious offices. This would be similar to "sir" or "mister" in English. In other places, "bishop" is used as a form of the highest respect for a religious or friar. In a letter, St. Francis refers to St. Anthony of Padua in this way, though he was never an ordained bishop.

Regarding St. Francis, there are other potentially confusing titles or references. He was (and still sometimes is) often referred to by his followers as "Father," even though he was an ordained deacon and never a priest; in this context, *Father* refers to his role as founder of the Franciscan Order. In other passages, he is frequently referred to as "blessed." This does not refer to the penultimate stage of the process of canonization; rather, it is a medieval religious title, indicating the state of highest divine favor and grace.

Lastly, in the Italian edition, pronouns referring to God were sometimes capitalized, while in other places, they were not. Here, I translated accordingly, even though it might appear incongruous.

Introduction to the Franciscan Legends

Traditionally, *Vitae* (Lives)—biographies, or more accurately, hagiographies—were written to accompany the canonizations of saints. They were also referred to as legends. This is not to say that they were myths; rather, the stories were "to be read," which is the etymological meaning of the word.

Virtually everything we know about St. Francis comes from the early Lives and Legends from the thirteenth and fourteenth centuries. The first was written just two years after Francis's death. In 1228, the same year in which Francis was canonized, the writing of his life story was entrusted by Pope Gregory IX to Thomas of Celano, an erudite friar and contemporary of St. Francis. Completed in early 1229, Thomas's work enjoys a special place in the annals of Franciscan history as the original *Vita* of St. Francis.

In the 1230s, other important Lives of St. Francis were recorded. The most notable was penned by Julian of Spire. However, he was from Germany, was educated in Paris, and never knew St. Francis. Moreover, his biography essentially repeated that of Thomas. Therefore, it never assumed the importance of Thomas's work. Another early work was *Sacred Exchange between St. Francis and Lady Poverty*. Written in the immediate years after Francis's death, it was not meant to be a biography. Instead, it was an allegory and spiritual exhortation, encouraging the friars to love and embrace poverty. Another early writing is commonly known as the *Anonymous of Perugia*, written in the late 1230s and completed before 1241. It was discovered in the seventeenth century in a Franciscan convent in Perugia, hence its name. It was most likely written by John of Perugia—a friar and close companion of Brother Giles, the third follower of Francis, and an acquaintance of Brother Bernard, the first follower. The object of his work was not so much the life of St. Francis but a history of the beginning of the Order.

Despite the proliferation of these early biographies, none of them ever reached the same prominence as Thomas's. For decades, the *First Life* of St. Francis was commonly accepted as the official biography, especially since it had the backing of the pope. However, there were weaknesses. Celano was not a close companion of Francis, and his biography was written too soon after the founder's death. It was riddled with gaps.

After the death of Pope Gregory IX, the criticism spilled out into the open. In 1244, during a general chapter in Genoa, the issue was taken up by the friars. The minister general, Crescentius of Jesi, sent out a letter to all the friars, asking those who had known Francis to submit their personal testimonies so that the gaps could be filled. The result was an influx of material. The inhabitants of Assisi shared their memories, challenging Thomas's narrative of the utter wickedness and depravity that prevailed in both the saint's family and Assisian society. John of Perugia's work was likely submitted at this time as well.

All this material was handed over to Thomas of Celano. He was commissioned not to write a fresh, new biography or replace the first one but to fill the gaps in his first work, which had been written almost twenty years earlier. Thus, his second work, *Remembrance of a Desire of a Soul* (commonly referred to as the *Second Life*), was a more thorough biography, as it depicted a more organized version of the life of the founder. When he completed it around 1247, he was asked to further perfect it by including miracles, which had somehow been omitted. The result was a third work, known as the *Treatise on Miracles of St. Francis.* The trilogy of works on St. Francis by Thomas of Celano remains foundational among all Lives of the saint.

By now, in the mid-thirteenth century, in addition to the official works of Thomas, more biographies of St. Francis began circulating. While some of the ones mentioned above were sound, there were other less reliable narratives.

By the time Bonaventure of Bagnoregio (1221–1274) was chosen as the seventh minister general of the Order of Friars Minor in 1257, an office he held until his death in 1274, the Order was facing serious challenges. Externally, the friars were engaged in a bitter struggle with the secular clergy regarding the mendicants' status in the universities and dioceses. Internally, there were heated tensions, particularly regarding observance of the Rule. As it was, two distinct camps of friars were emerging.

Before Francis died, the friars had been commissioned with more significant pastoral roles, and his original vision and form of life were being relaxed. As the Order aged and took on more apostolic works, it became more and more difficult to subsist on alms, practice manual labor, observe evangelical penance, and live in poor dwellings, all the while adhering to strict poverty. In order to achieve their ministries more practically, the "relaxed" friars (eventually known as the Conventuals) sought to mitigate the vigor of the Rule. On the other hand, there were those friars who sought to continue to imitate the life of the founder to the letter. Among these was a radical branch of friars who had been heavily influenced by the writings of Joachim of Fiore, a firebrand Cistercian abbot and mystic who prophesied that the age of the Spirit was near. Known as the Spirituals, many were promoting a version of St. Francis based on their conviction that the friars had an important role not just in the Church but in eschatological history and the end times.

With this turmoil roiling the Order, it was all the more necessary to capture the essence of St. Francis, especially as some within these factions were promoting a heavily slanted version of the founder to bolster their partisan positions. Thus, in 1260, Bonaventure was given the mandate to compose a new biography. It was a monumental task. In effect, Bonaventure was charged with creating a new Life of St. Francis that could unify the divergent camps within the Order.

St. Bonaventure (canonized in 1381) is regarded as one of the most important philosophers and theologians from the medieval Scholastic tradition. His writings include numerous commentaries, treatises, and reflections. His most well-known work is *Itinerarium mentis in Deum* (Journey of the mind into God), a spiritual masterpiece mapping the mystical ascent to God in a series of stages.

The result of Bonaventure's work of St. Francis—*Legenda maior Sancti Francisci* (Major legend of Saint Francis)—was another spiritual masterpiece. His work portrayed Francis as a man of perfect virtue, presented as a manifestation of grace and perfect conformity to Christ. As he was composing the complete Legend, he composed a shorter biography of the saint to be used in liturgical functions and readings. The secondary Legend is known as the *Minor Legend.*

Bonaventure's *Major Legend* was extremely well received by the other ministers of the Order, so much so that just six years after he wrote it, at the general chapter in Paris in 1266, a serious decision was taken: every Franciscan friary was ordered to destroy every biography of St. Francis in their libraries except one—that of Bonaventure of Bagnoregio. His biography was to be considered not just the *official* Life of St. Francis; it would be the *only* Life of St. Francis.

Happily, the older biographies survived, as Franciscan obedience did not extend to Benedictine or Augustinian libraries. Moreover, the collections of writings about St. Francis submitted after the 1244 general chapter in Genoa were cleverly determined not to be veritable biographies and were not destroyed. In any case, only ten years later, the ministers regretted the decision taken, and at the general chapter in Padua in 1276, they issued a counterorder: care should be taken to diligently collect and preserve every writing and biography related to the life of St. Francis.

In sum, Bonaventure's *Major Legend*—while certainly profoundly spiritually and theologically developed—was tamer and more sanitized when compared to the earlier biographies. Bonaventure's personal thoughts on grace, free will, virtue, and moral progress thoroughly inform his presentation of the life of Francis. Indeed, his Life of St. Francis was deeply influenced by his own journey and understanding of Christian spirituality. He spent a significant amount of time in a grotto in the mountain hermitage of Laverna, where he wrote *Itinerarium*. There, in the same spot where Francis received the stigmata, Bonaventure became convinced that the mystical conformity of St. Francis to the crucifix was not just a unique aspect of Francis's spiritual journey; it was fundamental to every Christian. Thus, the *Major Legend* is less a work by a historian and more that of a refined theologian who saw St. Francis and his role in the history of salvation: the founder of the Franciscan Order is the angel of the sixth seal[1], a true and veritable *alter Christus*.

Regarding Bonaventure's attempts at unifying the Order through his *Legend*, the verdict was mixed. While he shared some of the ideals of the Spirituals, for their leaders, he did not go nearly far enough in establishing St. Francis according to their understanding of the founder's unique place in eschatological history. They viewed St. Francis through an apocalyptic lens. He was the herald of a new era, appointed by God to usher in the "Age of the Spirit," and they, his followers, were part of this new age of holiness.

---

1 The sentence is from the Introduction to the "Fonti" in Italian. Though there is not a direction connection between the seals and angels in Revelation, it appears he is indicating St. Francis as one of the final angels playing a significant role in the end times and execution of God's plans. That is how the Spirituals, and Bonaventure, saw Francis's role in salvation history.

Given their radical fervor, the Spirituals frequently criticized the direction of the Order as having become too relaxed and institutionalized. Many in the ecclesiastical hierarchy, including bishops and popes, according to them, were also corrupt. Eventually, the Spirituals were condemned. Pope John XXII issued decrees against them, and some of their leaders were imprisoned and even executed for heresy.

The saga of the Spirituals is important in understanding the development of Lives of St. Francis from the second half of the thirteenth century to the first half of the fourteenth century. Their leaders, such as Ubertino of Casale, condemned Bonaventure's biography, accusing him of having omitted pertinent facts and sayings considered embarrassing or compromising to the leadership of the Order.

In 1305, after having been banished from Florence to Laverna for having criticized the pope, Ubertino wrote the *Tree of Crucified Life of Jesus*. He used the image of a tree as a central symbol to represent the life and crucifixion of Jesus. Writing under the mantle of mysticism and allusion, the work epitomizes the vision and thought of the Spirituals, based on Joachim of Fiore's apocalyptic writings. In Book Five, Ubertino introduces St. Francis. The founder is described in mystical and prophetic terms as having been generated by Jesus.

Ubertino wrote that Francis's unique privilege was to have "transmitted to holy Church the life of Jesus in the communal and durable form of his Order." Ubertino did not hold back from incessant polemic barbs against Franciscan ministers and institutional prelates.

A more even-handed work associated with the tradition of the Spirituals is the *Fioretti* (Little Flowers of St. Francis). Not remotely an intellectual treatise, it is a collection of popular legends and tales about the lives of Francis and the early friars narrated in an earthy, colloquial manner. In line with the spirituality of the Spirituals, it is replete with colorful anecdotes, supernatural visions and miracles, and examples of early Franciscan piety, many of which are situated in the remote, mountain hermitages. *The Little Flowers* was compiled by a friar in the region of the Marches, likely between 1328 and 1337. Perhaps due to the complete absence of polemics (with which Ubertino's work is replete), the *Fioretti* is considered a spiritual classic not just within the Franciscan Order but within Christendom itself.

A number of other texts were once associated with the Spirituals, though the opinion among scholars today has changed. Returning to the request of Crescentius from Jesi, who sought the submission of testimonies of the life of St. Francis from those who knew him, many of these texts were copied and conserved.

Perhaps the most valuable response was from three early companions of the saint who were residing in Greccio. We know who they were from a letter that accompanied their writings: Brothers Leo, Rufino, and Angelo. Today, the manuscript they sent is known as the *Legend of the Three Companions*, and it is considered one of the most important early Franciscan biographies.

Another important work that was submitted after Crescentius's request is known as the *Assisi Compilation*. It was traditionally known as the *Legend of Perugia*, since it was discovered in a library in Perugia in 1922. This work is not a biography; rather, it is a compilation of stories and anecdotes sent from those "who were with him." The texts were copied and originally preserved at the Sacred Convent in Assisi.

Another often-cited work associated with the Spirituals is the *Mirror of Perfection*. It was actually composed in 1318, though it was long believed that Brother Leo had penned it one century earlier. (The discrepancy is due to an error in Roman numerals.) The *Mirror of Perfection* consists of a collection of testimonies by those who knew St. Francis. Due to the choice of certain texts that were included, the work is considered part of the tradition of the Spirituals.

These latter texts present a portrait of St. Francis that differs considerably in style and content from the "official" biographies penned by Thomas of Celano and St. Bonaventure. They were not commissioned by a pope or the minister general with the task of being accepted as official biographies. Nor were they systematic examinations of the founder in light of a theological program. Instead, St. Francis is presented by his companions, many of whom were with him from the beginning. He comes across as authentic and real.

Unfortunately, since for a long time these works were considered expressions of the thought of the Spirituals, they were seen as the cause of the bitter struggle that consumed the Order for decades, if not centuries. For this reason, they were shunned. When these texts surfaced in dusty convent libraries in the eighteenth and nineteenth centuries, modern Franciscan historians (such as Paul Sabatier) believed that the true St. Francis had been rediscovered. These modern writers claimed that the portrait of St. Francis as depicted in the official Legends (that is, the works by Thomas of Celano and St. Bonaventure) had been compromised.

Today, the consensus among Franciscan scholars is that all the biographies are closer to one another than was previously believed. When examined critically—and taking into account the historical moment and by whom the works were created—each contains specific truths. Without a doubt, the early Legends—both the official ones and those written by Francis's close companions—taken together offer a thorough and authentic portrait of St. Francis.

Chronology

CONVERSION (1181–1208)

– 1181/1182: Born in Assisi and baptized with the name John. After his father returned from France, he renamed him Francesco.

– 1198–1200: After the death of Emperor Henry VI (September 1197), the commoners of Assisi destroy the imperial fortress of Assisi and attack the fortified houses of the nobility, many of whom take refuge in Perugia. Francis may have participated in the battle.

– November 1202: War breaks out between Perugia and Assisi, and Francis takes part. The army of Assisi is defeated in the battle of Collestrada.

– 1202–1203: Francis is imprisoned in Perugia for one year. He is released after his father pays a ransom.

– 1204: Francis suffers a long illness.

– Late 1204 or early 1205: Francis sets out to Puglia to fight again, this time in a crusade in southern Italy. In Spoleto, he has a mysterious vision-dream that causes him to change his plans, and he returns to Assisi. His gradual process of conversion begins.

– Summer 1205: Francis encounters a leper, representing the beginning of his penance (conversion), as he wrote in his *Testament*.

– Autumn 1205: In San Damiano, Christ speaks to Francis through the crucifix, telling him to rebuild the church. The conflict with his father begins.

– Early 1206: Summoned by the bishop of Assisi, Francis renounces his worldly inheritance before his father and the townspeople. He leaves Assisi, stopping at a monastery, where he works as a scullion. He continues to Gubbio, where he spends several months caring for lepers. There, he is given a habit by a friend.

– Summer 1206: Francis returns to Assisi donning a hermit's tunic, and he begins to repair the church of

San Damiano. There, he prophesies the arrival of the Poor Ladies.

– Summer 1206–early 1207: Francis repairs two more churches—San Pietro of Spina and Our Lady of the Angels (also known as the Portiuncula).

THE ORDER (1208–1215)

1208

– February 24, 1208 (Feast of St. Matthias): At Mass at the Portiuncula, Francis hears the Gospel in which Christ sends the apostles out with nothing. Receiving his vocation to poverty, he dons a rough habit and a chord and begins to announce penance.

– April 16: Bernard of Quintavalle is the first to follow Francis. Peter of Catanii also follows Francis.

– April 23: Brother Giles is received at the Portiuncula as a follower of Francis.

– Spring: The first mission. Giles and Francis go to the March of Ancona, while the other two go in another direction.

– Summer: Three more brothers join, including Philip the Long.

– Autumn 1208–early 1209: The second mission. Francis sends the friars two by two in the four directions of the world. Francis and a brother reach Poggio Bustone in the Rieti valley. After being assured of the remission of his sins and the future growth of the Order, Francis comforts and encourages his companions.

<u>1209</u>

– Spring: The friars return to the Portiuncula. More enter, now numbering twelve.

– Spring: Francis writes a brief *Rule of Life* "according to the form of the Holy Gospel" and presents it to Pope Innocent III, who approves it orally.

– Summer: On the way back to Assisi, the friars stop temporarily near Orte. Then, they settle in a hut in Rivotorto near Assisi.

– September: Emperor Otto IV passes Rivotorto.

– 1209 or 1210: Forced to leave Rivotorto, the fledgling group settles by the small church of St. Mary of the Angels (also known as the Portiuncula). After receiving permission from the Benedictine abbot of San Benedetto (whose Order owned the property), St. Mary of the Angels becomes the mother church of the Order.– 1209 or 1210: The beginning of the Third Order.

<u>1211 or 1212</u>

– Summer: Francis tries to reach Syria, but headwinds push the ship onto the coast of Dalmatia. Francis returns to Ancona.

<u>1212</u>

– March 18–19: On the night of Palm Sunday, Francis welcomes Clare at St. Mary of the Angels, gives her the tonsure, and vests her in a religious tunic.

– Summer: Francis returns to Rome to inform Innocent III on the developments of the Order. He meets Lady Jacopa dei Settesoli, a Roman noblewoman and benefactress of the Order.

1213

– May 8: In San Leo of Montefeltro, Count Orlando offers Francis the mountain of La Verna overlooking his territory of Chiusi.

– 1213 or 1214: Francis attempts to reach Morocco again in order to preach to the Muslims; he attempts the route by land from Spain, but an illness forces him to return to Assisi.

1215

– November: the Fourth Lateran Council takes place in Rome. Francis likely attends and possibly meets St. Dominic. Afterward, inspired by the teachings of the council, his "Eucharistic crusade" begins.

GROWTH (1216–1223)

1216

– July 16: Pope Innocent III dies in Perugia and is succeeded by Pope Honorius III.

– Late summer: Pope Honorius approves the Plenary Indulgence attached to the Portiuncula, also known as the Pardon of Assisi.

1217

– May 5: At the first general chapter, the friars initiate the first missions beyond "the Alps and the Seas" (that is, northern Europe and the Holy Land).

1218

– June 11, 1218: Honorius III publishes *Cum dilecti*, assuring bishops of the full catholicity of the Friars Minor.

1219

– May 26: At the Pentecost chapter, during the Fifth Crusade, a second mission of the friars beyond the Alps and Seas is decided. Friars leave for Germany, France, Hungary, and Spain. Five friars, led by Br. Berard, leave for the Holy Land.

– June 24: Francis sails from Ancona to Acre (Akko), in today's northern Israel, and then Damietta, where the Crusaders are deployed against the Muslim army.

– Autumn: Francis meets Sultan Malik-al-Kamil, where he is graciously welcomed. After he preaches the Gospel, there are no conversions, and Francis returns to the Crusader camp.

1220

– January: Br. Berard and the other friars are martyred in Morocco; they are known as the Franciscan Protomartyrs.

– Spring or summer: Informed that the "vicars" left in charge in Italy had introduced arbitrary provisions into the Rule, Francis returns to Italy via Venice. Cardinal Hugolino is appointed Protector of the Order.

– September 22: In his papal bull *Cum secundum*, Pope Honorius III directs the Franciscans to begin a one-year novitiate for new friars.

– 1220 (or 1217 or 1218): Francis renounces his role governing the Order, entrusting it to Peter Catanii as vicar.

1221

– March 10: Peter of Catanii dies, and Brother Elias is appointed vicar.

– May 30: Another general chapter, called the Chapter of Mats, takes place. A formal Rule is approved though not confirmed with the official papal bull. This unapproved Rule is known as the Rule of 1221.

– 1221: Pope Honorius III approves *Memoriale propositi*, which is considered the first Rule of the Order of Penitents—later called the Third Order of St. Francis and today the Secular Franciscan Order).

– 1221–1222: Francis preaches in southern Italy.

HOLINESS (1223–1228)

1223

– Early part of the year: Francis retreats to Fontecolombo with Brother Leo and Brother Bonizzo to draft the definitive Rule.

– June 11: The Rule is discussed at the general chapter and submitted to the pope for approval.

– November 29: Pope Honorius III formally approves the Rule with the bull *Solet annuere*. It is known as the Rule of 1223, or the Approved Rule.

– December 24–25: In Greccio, Francis serves Mass with live animals, creating the first creche, or nativity scene.

1224

– June 2: At the general chapter, it is decided to send friars to England.

– July or August: In Foligno, Brother Elias prophesies that Francis has two years to live.

– August 15–September 29: During a fast from the Assumption to the Feast of St. Michael, Francis receives the stigmata at Mount Laverna. The feast is observed on September 17, though it likely occurred on September 14.

– October–November: Francis returns to the Portiuncula, ministering in the upper Tiber Valley.

– December 1224–February 1225: Riding on a donkey, Francis preaches through Umbria and the March of Ancona.

1225

– March: At San Damiano, Francis's eye condition worsens. At the insistence of the bishop and Brother Elias, Francis consents to treatment, but weather is inclement and treatment is postponed.

– April–May: In San Damiano, Francis receives the divine promise of eternal life. The next morning, nearly blind, he composes the *Canticle of the Creatures.*

– June: Francis adds the “forgiveness” stanza to the *Canticle*, which leads to a reconciliation between the bishop and mayor of Assisi.

– June–July: Following a letter from Cardinal Hugolino, Francis goes to Rieti, where he meets the papal court.

– July–August: Urged by Cardinal Hugolino, Francis goes to Fonte Colombo to undergo eye treatment. A doctor cauterizes his temples, without improvement.

– September: Francis moves to San Fabiano near Rieti (today, it is the Sanctuary of La Foresta) for more doctor visits, all to no avail. He restores the trampled vineyard of the poor priest.

1226

– February 6: Francis leaves the Rieti Valley.

– April: Francis goes to Siena for further medical treatments; he dictates a brief testament.

– May–June: Francis goes to a hermitage near Cortona, referred to as the “Cells.”

– July–August: For respite from the summer heat, Francis is taken to Bagnara, in the mountains east of Assisi.

– Late August or early September: Francis's condition worsens, and he is taken first to the castle settlement of Nottiano, then to the bishop's palace in Assisi. At the announcement of his approaching death, he dictates the last stanza of his Canticle.

– September: Sensing that death is near, Francis is taken to the Portiuncula. He stops to bless the city. Around this time, he dictates his final *Testament*.

– October 3: Francis dies at the Portiuncula after sunset on Saturday, October 3, or, according to the medieval liturgical computation, on Sunday, October 4.

– October 4: Francis's body is transported to Assisi. On the way, the procession stops in San Damiano so St. Clare and the sisters can pay homage to him. Then he is buried in the church of San Giorgio, now incorporated into the Basilica of St. Clare.

– October: Brother Elias writes a letter to all the friars, informing them of Francis's death and reception of the stigmata.

1227

– March 19: Cardinal Hugolino, the Protector of the Franciscan Order and personal friend of Francis, is elected pope, taking the name Gregory IX.

1228

– July 16: Pope Gregory IX comes to Assisi to preside over the canonization of Saint Francis.

– July 19: Pope Gregory publishes the papal bull *Mira circa nos,* confirming the inscription of St. Francis in the Register of Saints and the celebration of his feast on October 4.

1229

– February 25: Pope Gregory IX approves Thomas of Celano's first biography of the saint, the *Life of Blessed Francis* (today known as the *First Life*), which the same pontiff had commissioned.

1230

– May 25: St. Francis's remains are translated from San Giorgio to the basilica erected in his honor. His relics remain there today.

Prologue

April 29, AD 1228

The pope entrusts Thomas of Celano with the task of writing the Vita, *or First Life of St. Francis.*

At the invitation of the glorious Lord Pope Gregory, I have undertaken to diligently narrate the deeds and life of our most blessed Father, Francis. I have tried to do so orderly and with devotion, always choosing truth as my teacher and guide. But since no one can retain by heart all of his works and teachings, I have limited myself to faithfully transcribing at least those things that I myself have gathered from his own voice or learned from the accounts of tried and sincere witnesses, setting them down in the best way that was possible to me, although so inferior to the merit of the subject. Would that I could truly be a worthy disciple of him who constantly avoided difficult language and the ornaments of rhetoric![2]

2 Celano, *First Life*, 315.

Part I: Conversion

In the World

Winter AD 1181–1182

Pica was nearing the end of her term. Her relatives and the women of the neighborhood were looking after her, as all joyfully anticipated the birth of her first child. Her husband, Pietro [di Bernardone], was in France dealing with commercial interests. However, when her term came to pass, the women became anxious and began to fear for Pica's health. Then suddenly, a mysterious pilgrim came to the door of the house, bearing a message for the young expectant mother: She would be able to deliver only in a stable. At that, Pica was taken to the family stable next to the house, where, among an ox and a donkey, she gave birth to a son.[3]

3 From a fifteenth-century legend.

AD 1182

Baptized by his mother with the name John, his father calls him Francis.

Born in the city of Assisi, in the area of the Spoleto Valley, he was first called John [after the Baptist] by his mother, then Francesco by his father [who had been away in worldly France], and certainly, as to the sound, he kept the name imposed by his father, but as to the meaning, he also fulfilled that given by his mother.[4]

Therefore, the name John is appropriate to the mission that he later carried out, while that of Francis [is appropriate] instead to his fame, which soon spread everywhere after his complete conversion to God. Beyond the feast of any other saint, he considered most solemn that of John the Baptist, whose illustrious name had impressed on his soul a sign of arcane power.[5]

Francis is known for generosity but not obedience to God.

In his youth, he was brought up in vanities, among the vain sons of men. After a summary education, he was destined for the lucrative business of commerce.

---

4 Bonaventure, *Minor Legend*, 1330.
5 Celano, *Second Life*, 583.

Yet, through divine assistance and protection, he did not follow the unbridled instincts of the flesh, although [he was] among licentious youths. Moreover, although [he was] among merchants intent on gain, he did not place his hope in money and treasures.[6]

Vivid as he was with intelligence, he began to practice his father's profession, the cloth trade, though in a completely different manner. Francis was much more cheerful and generous, given to playing games. He would wander around Assisi day and night with a group of likeminded friends. He was so liberal in spending that he would squander all the money he earned or could acquire on feasts and other things. For this reason, his parents scolded him for his excessive spending on himself and others, as if he were the descendant of some great prince rather than the son of merchants. But since they were wealthy and they loved him dearly, they let him carry on in that behavior, not wanting to sadden him. His mother, when she heard the neighbors talking about the young man's prodigality, would answer, "What do you think of my son? He will be a son of God yet, by His grace."

---

6 Bonaventure, *Minor Legend*, 1330.

He was not only a spendthrift in dining and entertainment, but he also went beyond all limits in his dress. He had more sumptuous clothes made than were appropriate [according to his social position]. In his quest for originality, he was so vain that he would sometimes sew precious fabrics and coarse cloth together in the same garment. All the same, by nature, he was gentle in his behavior and manner of speaking. And following a choice born of conviction, he addressed no one with insulting or foul words. On the contrary, although he was a shining and dissipated young person, he was determined not to respond to those who initiated lewd discourse. Thus his fame spread throughout almost the entire region, and many who knew him predicted that he would accomplish something great.[7]

The hand of the Lord rested upon him, and the right hand of the Most High would transform him, so that, through him, sinners might rediscover the hope of living again in grace, and he might remain for all an example of conversion to God.[8]

---

7 *Legend of the Three Companions*, 1396–1397.

8 Celano, *First Life*, 321.

November AD 1202

Francis fights on behalf of Assisi against Perugia and is imprisoned for one year.

During the battle between Perugia and Assisi, Francis was captured with many of his fellow citizens and taken prisoner to Perugia. Being noble in manner [and dress], they locked him in prison together with the knights.

At a certain point, while his fellow prisoners were sad and dejected, Francis, cheerful and jovial by nature, did not seem sad but cheerful. One of his companions then told him that he was foolish to act cheerful while in prison. But Francis countered in a vibrant voice, "What do you think of me? You all should know that I will be adored throughout the world."

A knight of his group insulted one of his fellow prisoners. For this reason, all the others sought to isolate him. But Francis continued to befriend him, exhorting everyone to do the same. After one year, peace was negotiated between Perugia and Assisi, and Francis returned to Assisi together with his fellow prisoners.[9]

---

9 *Legend of the Three Companions*, 1398.

Francis encounters a poor man in his shop.

One day, he was in the shop where he sold fabrics, completely absorbed in thoughts related to such business affairs, when a poor man appeared asking for alms for the love of God. Intent on dreams of wealth, Francis sent him away without giving him anything. As the beggar walked away, the young man [Francis], touched by divine grace, began to reproach himself as a villain for his great wrongdoing, saying to himself, "If that poor man had asked for a contribution in the name of some count or great baron, you would certainly have given him what he asked. How much more should you have done so, since he asked in the name of the King of kings and the Ruler of the universe?" For this reason, he resolved in his heart that from then on, he would refuse nothing that was asked of him in the name of such a great Lord. And calling the poor man, he gave him alms generously.[10]

A poor man pays homage to Francis in the streets.

There was a very simple man from Assisi who was educated, as is believed, by God. Every time he met Francis in the streets of the city, he took off his cloak

10 *Anonymous of Perugia*, 1490.

and spread it at his feet, proclaiming that Francis was worthy of all veneration because soon he would accomplish great things, for which he would be honored and glorified by all Christians.[11]

Francis encounters a poor knight in the streets.

One day, Francis met a poor and nearly naked knight. Moved by compassion, out of love of Christ, he generously gave him the well-kept clothes he was wearing. Was his gesture less than that of the most holy St. Martin [who divided his cloak with a sword to give half to a poor man]? The deed and generosity were the same, only the manner is different: Francis gives his clothes before the rest, while the other gives them at the end, after having renounced everything. Both lived poorly and humbly in this world but entered Heaven rich. That one—a knight but poor—clothed a poor man with part of his clothes; this one—not a knight but rich—clothed a poor knight with all of his clothes. Both, for having fulfilled the command of Christ, merited being visited by Christ in a vision, who praised the one for the perfection he had achieved and invited the

11 Bonaventure, *Major Legend*, 1029.

other [that is, Francis], with great kindness, to complete in himself what he still lacked.[12]

AD 1203

Francis is struck with a long illness.

But Francis still did not yet know God's plans for him. Busy with his [earthly] father's will in external activities and dragged downward by our nature corrupt from its origin, he had not yet learned to contemplate celestial realities, nor had he become accustomed to savoring divine realities. And since fear makes one understand the lesson, the hand of the Lord came upon him, and the intervention of the right hand of the Most High struck his body with long infirmities in order to render his soul disposed to the anointing of the Holy Spirit.[13]

AD 1204

[Struck by a long illness,] he began effectively to reason differently from the usual way. When he had recovered a little, to regain his strength, he began to

12 Celano, *Second Life*, 585.

13 Bonaventure, *Major Legend*, 1030.

walk around the house here and there with the aid of a cane. One day, he went out and admired the surrounding countryside more attentively. But the beauty of the fields and the pleasantness of the vineyards—all that is pleasant to look at—no longer delighted him anymore. He was astonished at this sudden change and considered all those who have their hearts attached to goods of this kind to be foolish.

From that day on, Francis began to take no account of himself and to consider with a certain contempt that which he had previously admired and loved—not, however, in a perfect and real way, because he was not yet free from the bonds of vanity, nor had he completely shaken off the yoke of perverse slavery. To abandon habits is indeed very difficult. Once they have taken root in the soul, they are not easily uprooted. The spirit, even after distancing [vices] far away, returns to its primitive attitudes, and vice mostly ends up becoming second nature. Therefore, Francis still seeks to remove himself from the divine hand. Almost forgetful of his Father's correction, with fortune smiling upon him, he caresses earthly thoughts. Unaware of the will of God, he still promises to achieve great feats for worldly vainglory.[14]

---

14 Celano, *First Life*, 323–324.

Late AD 1204

Francis prepares for battle a second time.

After a few years [after the battle with Perugia], a nobleman from Assisi, eager to acquire money and glory, prepares to go to war and fight in Puglia [in southern Italy]. When Francis hears this, he is in turn seized by the desire to accompany him. Thus, to be knighted by a certain Count Gentile, he prepares a trousseau of precious garments; because, although he is less wealthy than that fellow citizen, he is still more generous in spending.[15]

Francis has a dream but misinterprets it.

One night in which he had applied himself with all determination to the accomplishment of this project and was burning with desire to depart, He Who had struck him with the rod of justice visited him in a dream with the sweetness of grace. And since he was avid for glory, He conquered and exalted him with the same mirage of glory. It seemed that he saw his house full of weapons: saddles, shields, spears, and other instruments of war. And he greatly rejoiced at this,

---

15 *Legend of the Three Companions*, 1399.

wondering in amazement what it was all for. His gaze was not accustomed to the sight of those instruments in the house but rather to piles of cloth to be sold. And while he was greatly surprised at the unexpected event, he heard a voice say that all those weapons were for him and his soldiers.[16]

When he awoke in the morning, he thought he understood that this unusual vision was a premonition of glory for him. Indeed, his mind was not yet trained to scrutinize divine mysteries, and he did not yet know how to intuit the truth of invisible things through the appearances of visible things.[17]

[He was] taken up with the worldly thought (he had not yet fully tasted the spirit of God) that he would become a great prince. Taking it as an omen of exceptional fortune, he decided to leave for Puglia to be knighted by that count. He was so much more radiant than usual, that to many who appeared surprised and asked where he was getting so much joy, he replied, "I know that I will become a great prince."[18]

---

16 Celano, *First Life*, 326–327.

17 Bonaventure, *Major Legend*, 1031.

18 *Legend of the Three Companions*, 1399.

Obedience

Having hired a squire, he mounted his horse and headed towards Puglia. Once he arrived in Spoleto, worried about the journey, at night he lay down to sleep. Then in his half-sleep, he heard a voice asking him where he was going, to whom Francis revealed his entire plan in order.[19]

Francis hears the voice again, interprets it correctly, and returns to Assisi.

The voice then asked him whom he thought could be more useful to Him: the servant or the master.

"The master," Francis replies.

"So then," the voice resumes, "why do you seek the servant instead of the Master?"

---

19 *Anonymous of Perugia*, 1492.

"What do you want me to do, O Lord?" asked Francis.

"Return," the Lord answered him, "to your native land, because through my work your vision will be spiritually fulfilled."

Francis returned to Assisi without delay, now made a model of obedience and transformed by the denial of his will, as from Saul to Paul. He was thrown to the ground and under the harsh blows spoke sweet words; Francis instead changed worldly weapons into spiritual ones, and in place of military glory, he received a divine investiture. Thus, to those—and there were many—who were amazed at his unusual joy, he replied that he would become a great prince.[20]

Francis loses interest in worldly merriments.

He began to transform himself into a perfect man, completely different from the one he had been before. But once he had returned home, the sons of Babylon began to follow him again. Although against his will, they dragged him down a path very different from the one he intended to follow. The company of young people of Assisi who had once had him as a guide in their

20 Celano, *Second Life*, 587.

levity began once again to invite him to banquets, in which they constantly indulged in debauchery and vulgarity. They elected him king of the feast because they knew from experience that, in his generosity, he would have paid the expenses for everyone. They became his subjects in order to feed themselves and agreed to obey in order to be satiated. Francis did not refuse the honor offered to him, so as not to be branded as avaricious; while continuing in his devout meditations, he did not forget courtesy. He prepared a sumptuous banquet with an abundance of exquisite foods. Then, when they were stuffed to the point of vomiting, they poured out into the squares of the city, dirtying them with their drunken songs. Francis followed them, holding the scepter in his hand like a lord.[21]

Then, suddenly, the Lord visited him, and his heart was filled with such sweetness that he could not move or speak. And he could not hear or perceive anything other than that sweetness that had estranged him from every physical sensation, so much so that (as he himself later confided) he could not have moved from that place even if they had torn him to shreds.

---

21 Celano, *Second Life*, 588.

His friends, turning around and seeing him so far away, returned to him, and they were astonished to see him transformed almost into another man. They asked him, "What were you thinking about, such that you did not follow us? Were you perhaps dreaming of taking a wife?"

He answered enthusiastically, "It is true. I was dreaming of taking as my wife the noblest, richest, and most beautiful spouse you have ever seen." And they began to laugh at him. But Francis said this not on his own initiative but inspired by God. In truth, his spouse was religious life that he embraced, made more noble, rich, and beautiful by poverty.[22]

Truly wonderful is the goodness of the Lord. He bestows magnificent gifts on those who perform the humblest actions; He saves and leads to progress, even in the whirlpools of the flood, what belongs to Him. Christ in fact fed the crowds with loaves and fishes; He did not refuse sinners His table. When they asked for Him as king, He fled and went up the mountain to pray. These are mysteries of God, which Francis strives toward. And even without knowing it, he is led to perfect wisdom.[23]

---

22 *Legend of the Three Companions*, 1402.

23 Celano, *Second Life*, 588.

Spring AD 1205

From then on, withdrawing from the noise of commerce and people, he devoutly supplicated divine clemency to deign to show him what he was to do. Meanwhile, the assiduous practice of prayer cultivated in him the flame of heavenly desires, and the love of the heavenly Homeland made him despise all earthly things as nothing. He felt that he had discovered that hidden treasure, and as a wise merchant, he sought to purchase that precious pearl he had found at the price of everything he possessed. But he did not yet know how to accomplish this. An inner prompting only made him understand that spiritual commerce must begin with contempt for the world and that the knight of Christ must begin with victory over oneself.[24]

Francis prays in secluded places with a companion.

Gradually freeing himself from the noise of the world, he strived to hide in the depths of his heart Christ Jesus. [. . .] Often and almost every day, he immersed himself secretly in prayer. He was also driven to all this in a certain way by that mysterious sweetness

---

24 Bonaventure, *Major Legend*, 1033.

that, visiting him more and more often in his soul, urged him to pray even when he was in the square or in other public places.[25]

There was a young man in Assisi whom Francis loved more than the others. Since he was a peer and their friendship and mutual affection invited him to trust him with his secrets, Francis led him with him to solitary places suitable for spiritual recollection, where [Francis] revealed to him that he had discovered a great and precious treasure. The friend, exultant and intrigued, always gladly accepted the invitation to accompany him.

On the outskirts of the city there was a cave, where they often went and talked about this treasure. The man of God, already a saint by desire of being one, entered it, leaving his companion waiting outside. Filled with unusual new fervor, he prayed to his Father in secret. He rejoiced that no one knew what was happening within him, and wisely concealing the best for the greater good, he asked counsel of God alone regarding his holy purposes. He devoutly beseeched the eternal and true God to show him his way and to teach him how to fulfill his will. A tremendous struggle

---

25 *Legend of the Three Companions*, 1403.

was taking place within him, and he could not be at peace until he had fulfilled what he had set out to do. A thousand thoughts assailed him and caused him great suffering with their persistence.

He burned inwardly with divine fire and could not conceal externally the fervor of his soul. He deplored his grave sins—the offenses committed in the eyes of the divine majesty. By now, vanities of the past and present no longer attracted him, though he felt unsure of being able to resist them in the future. It is therefore understandable that, when he returned to his companion, he was so exhausted as to appear different from how he had entered [the cave].[26]

While he was frequenting secluded places, which he felt were suitable for prayer, the devil tried to drive him away through malicious cunning. He depicted in Francis's heart a fellow citizen of Assisi—a monstrously hunchbacked woman. She had such an appearance that she aroused horror in everyone. He threatened Francis to make him like her if he did not abandon his intentions. But comforted by the Lord, his response was joyful, full of grace and salvation. God said to him in spirit, "Francis, now leave worldly and vain pleasures

26 Celano, *First Life*, 329.

for spiritual ones. Prefer bitter things to sweet ones, and despise yourself if you wish to know me. Because you will taste what I tell you, even if the order is turned upside down." Immediately, he felt led to follow the command of the Lord and spurred to put himself to the test.[27]

Francis's love for poverty and the poor deepens. He goes to Rome on pilgrimage.

He firmly resolved never to refuse alms to the poor who asked for them out of love of God but on the contrary to give more spontaneously and generously than usual. To every poor person who asked for charity when Francis was away from home, he provided money; if he did not have any, he gave him his hat or belt, so as not to send him away empty handed. If he did not have these things, he withdrew to the side, took off his shirt, and secretly gave it to the poor person, begging him to take it out of love of God. Moreover, he bought items for the decorum of churches, which he secretly gave to poor priests.

In the absence of his father, when Francis remained at home, even if he took meals only with his mother,

27 Celano, *Second Life*, 591.

he filled the table with bread, as if he were preparing for the entire family. His mother asked him why he was piling up all those loaves, to which he answered that it was to give alms to the poor, since he had decided to aid anyone who asked out of love of God. His mother, who loved him more tenderly than her other children, allowed him to do these things, observing what he was doing and feeling great amazement in her heart.

Previously, he had been fond of joining the brigade of his friends when they invited him, and he loved their company so much that he would leave the table as soon as he had a bite, leaving his family members saddened by his inconsiderate departure. Now, however, his heart was intent solely on seeing the poor or knowing to whom he should bestow aid more generously.

Divine grace had profoundly changed him. Although he was still wearing worldly clothing, he longed to remain unknown in some city, where he could exchange his clothes for the rags of a beggar so he could try begging alms for himself for the love of God.

It happened at that time that Francis went to Rome on a pilgrimage. Upon entering the Basilica of St. Peter, he noticed how stingy some of the donations were. He asked himself, "If the Prince of the Apostles should be honored with splendor, then why are these stingy people leaving such paltry offerings in this basilica, where [St. Peter's] body rests?" In a burst of fervor, he put his hand into his purse and took out a handful of silver coins, which when he threw over the grate of the altar, made such a lively jingling sound that all those present were astonished by such a magnificent offering.

When he came out, he stopped in front of the doors of the basilica, where many poor people were begging, and he secretly exchanged his clothes with those of a beggar. There, on the steps of the church, among the other beggars, he asked for alms in French. He spoke this language very fondly, although he did not speak it correctly. He then took off those miserable clothes, put on his own, and returned to Assisi.

There, he began to pray to the Lord to guide his path. He insisted in prayer that the Lord would reveal to him his vocation. However, he confided his secret to no one, nor did he avail himself of the counsel of anyone, except God alone, who had begun to guide his path, and sometimes the bishop of Assisi. At that time, in fact, no one followed the true poverty that Francis desired above everything else in the world, with the will to live and die in it.[28]

---

28 *Legend of the Three Companions*, 1403–1406.

One day, while he was praying fervently to the Lord, he heard Him say, "Francis, if you wish to know My will, you must despise and hate everything that you loved in the world and desired to possess. When you have begun to do this, what was once attractive and sweet to you will seem unbearable and bitter, and you will draw great sweetness and immense delight from the things that you once abhorred."[29]

Fall AD 1205

In a pivotal moment, Francis embraces a leper.

Among all the horrors of human misery, Francis felt an instinctive repugnance toward lepers. But behold, one day he met one of them while he was riding his horse near Assisi. He felt great disgust at his appearance, but in order not to fail in his promised fidelity, as if transgressing an order received, he leaped from his horse and ran to kiss the man. The leper, who had stretched out his hand as if to receive something, received at the same time money and a kiss. Francis then remounted his horse and looked here and there—the

29 *Legend of the Three Companions*, 1407.

countryside was open and free all around from obstacles—but he no longer saw the leper.[30]

After a few days, Francis took a large sum of money and went to the leper hospital. He gathered them all together and distributed alms to each one, kissing their hands. Upon his return, that which had previously been repulsive to him—that is, the sight and touch of lepers—was truly transformed into sweetness. Francis himself confided that looking at lepers had previously been so unpleasant that not only did he refuse to look at them, he could not even bear to go near their dwellings. [Previously,] if he happened to pass by their homes or see one of them, although moved by compassion to give alms through an intermediary, he always turned his face away and held his nose. But by the grace of God, he became a companion and friend of the lepers so much that, as he stated in his *Testament*, God led him among them, and he served them humbly.[31]

---

30 Celano, *Second Life*, 592.

31 *Legend of the Three Companions*, 1408–1409.

January AD 1206

The crucifix of San Damiano speaks to Francis.

As he was passing near the church of San Damiano, he was told in spirit to go in and pray. Having gone in, he began to pray fervently before an image of the Crucifix.[32]

Francis makes the following prayer before the Crucifix:

Most High, glorious God,
illuminate the darkness of my heart,
and give me right faith,
certain hope, and perfect charity,
sense and knowledge, Lord,
that I may carry out your holy
and true commandment,
Amen.[33]

He bows down in supplication and devotion before the Crucifix and, touched in an extraordinary way by divine grace, finds himself completely changed. While he was thus deeply moved, suddenly—*Mirabile*

32 *Legend of the Three Companions*, 1411.

33 St. Francis, *Prayer of before the Crucifix*, 276.

dictu!—the image of Christ Crucified spoke to him from the painting and even moved its lips.

"Francis," he said, calling him by name, "go, repair my house, which as you see, is completely in ruins."

Francis, trembling and full of amazement, almost lost consciousness at these words. But he immediately set out to obey and concentrated solely on this invitation.[34]

From that moment on, the memory of Christ's passion was so vividly impressed on the inmost depths of his heart that whenever the crucifixion of Christ came to mind, he could barely hold back, even outwardly, from tears and sighs, as he later privately recalled when death was approaching. The man of God understood that through this vision, God was revealing to him the meaning of that Gospel passage, "Whoever wishes to come after me must deny himself, take up his cross, and follow me" (Mt 16:24).[35]

At the astonishing exhortation of that wonderful voice, the man of God was at first terrified. Then, filled with joy and admiration, he promptly arose and devoted himself entirely to carrying out the task of repairing the external edifice of the church. But the

34 Celano, *Second Life*, 593.

35 Bonaventure, *Major Legend*, 1035.

principal intention of the Voice was directed at the [universal] Church, which Christ purchased with the precious exchange of His blood, as the Holy Spirit would teach him and he himself would later reveal to his close companions.[36]

Francis sells his father's cloth to rebuild the church.

Prepared in such a way and confirmed by the Holy Spirit, the blessed servant of the Most High, since the appointed hour had struck, then followed the happy impulse of the soul. Trampling underfoot the goods of this world, he ran to the conquest of better goods. [. . .]

Francis, therefore, jumped to his feet, made the sign of the cross, prepared a horse, mounted it, and taking with him scarlet cloth to sell, quickly went to Foligno. There, according to his custom, he sold all the goods, and with a stroke of luck, even the horse! [. . .]

Approaching Assisi, he came across a church on the edge of the road built in ancient times and dedicated to San Damiano, which at that time was in a state of imminent ruin due to its old age. The new soldier of Christ approached the church and, moved by pity due to its miserable condition, entered it with reverential

36 Bonaventure, *Minor Legend*, 1334.

fear. Upon meeting a poor priest, he kissed his consecrated hands with great faith, offered him the money he had with him, and told him his intentions. Astonished and amazed by the sudden change of heart, the priest could not believe what he heard. Fearing a hoax, he refused to take the money. In fact, he had seen him recently making merry with his relatives and friends, surpassing everyone in foolishness. But Francis insisted and repeatedly beseeched the priest to believe him. He begged him to welcome him so he could serve the Lord with him. Finally, the priest allowed Francis to stay with him, although he persisted in refusing the money out of fear of Francis's relatives. Then Francis, a true despiser of wealth, threw it over a little window, caring for it as much as dust. He desired to possess wisdom, which is better than gold, and to obtain prudence, which is more precious than silver.[37]

The conflict between Francis and his father is exacerbated.

While the servant of the Most High was living in that place [San Damiano], like a diligent scout, his father went everywhere in search of news of his son.

37 Celano, *First Life*, 332–335.

When he learned that Francis was living there and in that manner, he was deeply grieved and shocked by the unexpected turn. He gathered his neighbors and friends and hastened to that place where the servant of God was. But he, who was still a novice in the battles of Christ, had anticipated their coming. Upon hearing the cries of his persecutors, he wished to give free reign to their anger by hiding in an underground refuge that he had prepared precisely in the event of such a threat.

For an entire month, he remained hidden in that pit, which was under the house and was known to perhaps only one person. He did not dare to come out except for absolute necessity. In the darkness of this cave, he ate the food that was offered to him from time to time, and all aid was given to him secretly. With burning tears, he implored God to free him from the hands of those who persecuted his soul and to grant him the grace to fulfill his promises. In fasting and weeping, he invoked the clemency of the Savior and, distrusting himself, placed all his trust in God.[38]

Feeling so filled with great joy, he began to reproach himself for his pusillanimity and cowardice. Leaving

---

38 Celano, *First Life*, 336.

his hiding place and banishing his fear, he faced the journey toward Assisi.

His fellow citizens watched him from the streets. Seeing his face so squalid and his spirit so changed, they believed he was out of his mind, and they threw mud and stones at him that they collected from the streets. They shouted and yelled at him, insulting him as if he were mad or demented. But the servant of God was not deterred or disturbed by their insults, and he passed among them as if deaf to everything.[39]

News of what was happening spread through the squares and streets of the city and reached the ears of his father. Upon hearing how his fellow citizens were mistreating him, Pietro immediately set out to get him. His intention was not to free Francis but to finish him off. Beside himself, he pounced on Francis like a wolf on a sheep. Staring at him with scowling eyes and a face disfigured by fury, he seized Francis and dragged him home. He locked him in a dark storeroom for several days, during which time, he did everything he could, with words and blows, to bring him back to worldly vanity. Francis did not allow himself to be influenced by words, nor by chains or beatings. He bore everything

39 Bonaventure, *Major Legend*, 1041.

with patience, becoming even more eager and strong in following his holy plan.[40]

It happened that urgent business obliged his father to be absent from home for a period, and the servant of God remained tied up in the family storeroom. Francis's mother, remaining alone with him and disapproving of her husband's method, spoke tenderly to her son. However, once she realized that nothing could dissuade him from his choice, his mother felt moved for him in the depths of her heart. Therefore, she loosened his bonds and freed him. After thanking Almighty God, Francis did not waste a second, and he returned to the place where he had been staying before. He now had greater freedom, and tried by the temptations and numerous struggles, he appeared more serene. Adversity had made his soul more tempered, and he went everywhere free and with greater firmness.[41]

Early AD 1206

Meanwhile, Pietro returned home and, discovering that his son was gone, began to insult his wife, thus adding sin upon sin. He then hurried to the municipal hall

40 *Legend of the Three Companions*, 1417–1418.

41 Celano, *First Life*, 341.

to lodge a complaint against his son, asking the consuls to intervene and force Francis to return the money he had taken from him, impoverishing his house. Seeing him in such an agitated state, the consuls sent a herald to the young man with a summons. But Francis replied to the herald that he was free by the grace of God and that he was a servant of the only God Most High and, as such, was no longer under the jurisdiction of the consuls. Not wanting to resort to violence, the consuls said to Pietro, "Since your son has consecrated himself to the service of God, he is no longer under our jurisdiction." Seeing that his appeal to the consuls had come to nothing, Pietro then went to the bishop of the city to file a complaint.[42]

That carnal father then sought to induce that son of grace, now stripped of money, to present himself before the bishop of the city, in order to make him renounce his entire paternal inheritance into his hands along with everything else he had. The true lover of poverty readily accepted the proposal.[43]

42 *Legend of the Three Companions*, 1418–1419.

43 Bonaventure, *Major Legend*, 1043.

Francis faces his father before the bishop of Assisi.

Francis came to the bishop's residence and was received by him with great joy. The bishop said to him, "Your father is angry with you and very upset because of you. Therefore, if you wish to be a servant of God, give him back the money you have with you, which is perhaps ill acquired, and as such, God does not want you to spend it for the benefit of the Church because of the sins of your father, whose anger will cool down in part if he recovers his money. Trust in the Lord, my son. Act with courage and do not be afraid, for the Most High will be your helper, and he will give to you in abundance what is necessary for the work of the Church."

The man of God stood up, happy and comforted by the bishop's words. Bringing the money before him, he said, "Lord, I wish to return to him with all my heart not only the money I received from selling his goods but also his clothes." Francis then went into the bishop's chamber and took off all his clothes and placed the money on top of them. Then he emerged naked in the presence of the bishop, his father, and all those present and said, "Listen, everyone, and understand. Up to now, I have called Pietro di Bernardone my father. But since I have made it my life's purpose to serve God, I give him back the money for which he was so troubled, as well as all the clothing that is from him. And from now on, I wish to say, 'Our Father, who art in Heaven' and no longer '[my] father, Pietro di Bernardone.'"[44]

Upon witnessing this and admiring the man of God in his boundless fervor, the bishop immediately rose up, took Francis weeping into his arms and, merciful and good as he was, covered him with his own pallium. He then instructed his attendants to give the young man something with which to cover himself. They offered him the poor and coarse cloak of a peasant, who was the servant of the bishop. Receiving it with gratitude, Francis took up a piece of chalk and traced the sign of the cross on it with his own hand, thus making it a garment suitable for covering a crucified, half-naked, poor man. Thus, the servant of the Most High King was left naked, so that he might follow the crucified naked Lord, the object of his love. Thus, he was provided with a cross, so that he might entrust his soul to the wood of salvation, saving himself from the shipwreck of the world by the cross.[45]

---

44 *Legend of the Three Companions*, 1419.

45 Bonaventure, *Major Legend*, 1043.

In the Spirit

On the way to Gubbio, Francis is attacked by robbers.

He who once adorned himself in purple gowns now went through a forest dressed in rags and singing the praises of God in French. Suddenly, scoundrels descended upon him, asking him brutishly who he was. The man of God answered fearlessly and confidently, "I am the herald of the great King. What is it to you?" They beat him and threw him into a pit full of snow, saying, "Stay there, you loutish herald of God!" But Francis, looking around and shaking off the snow, as soon as the robbers disappeared, leaped out of the pit and joyfully began to sing in a loud voice again, filling the forest with praises to the Creator of all things.

Finally, he arrived at a [Benedictine] monastery, where he remained for a number of days, dressed solely in a poor singlet and working as a scullion in the kitchen. For food, he was reduced to asking for at least a little broth. But finding no piety or even some old clothes, he left again, not out of disdain but of necessity, and he went to the city of Gubbio.[46]

Spring AD 1206

[In Gubbio,] he was recognized and welcomed by an old friend [named Spadalunga], who clothed him in a poor tunic, as a poor man of Christ. Then, a lover of every form of humility, Francis moved to the lepers, staying with them and serving them all, for God, with the greatest care. He washed their feet, bandaged their wounds, removed the rot from their wounds, and cleaned them of purulence. Moved by admirable devotion, he—who would soon become the Good Samaritan of the Gospel—also kissed their gangrenous wounds. For this reason, the Lord granted him great power and wonderful efficacy in healing in a wondrous way the diseases of the spirit and body.[47]

---

46 Celano, *First Life*, 346–347.

47 Bonaventure, *Major Legend*, 1045.

Summer AD 1206 to early AD 1208

Francis returns to Assisi to begin rebuilding churches.

Now well-rooted in the humility of Christ, Francis recalls the obedience to restore the church of San Damiano that the Cross had imposed on him. Truly obedient, he returns to Assisi to carry out the order of the divine voice, if only by begging. Casting aside all shame for the love of the poor Crucifix, he goes to seek alms from those with whom he had once lived in abundance, and he subjects his weak body, stooped over from fasting, to the weight of stones.[48]

He did not intend to build a new church but restore an ancient and ruined one. He did not level the foundation; rather, he built on it, thus leaving, unknowingly, the primacy to Christ. For no one could build another foundation other than that which has already been laid: Jesus Christ. Therefore, having returned to the place where, as has been said, the church of San Damiano had been built in ancient times, with the grace of the Most High, he quickly repaired it with complete diligence.[49]

---

48 Bonaventure, *Major Legend*, 1047.

49 Celano, *First Life*, 350.

[While residing at San Damiano,] the Lord enriched that poor and despised young man and filled him with the Holy Spirit. He placed the word of life in his mouth so that he would preach and announce to the people judgment and mercy, punishment and glory, recalling to their minds God's commandments, which they had forgotten. The Lord made him prince over the multitude of peoples, whom God, through him, gathered into unity from all over the world. The Lord led him along the straight and narrow way in that he did not wish to possess gold, silver, money, or anything else; rather, he followed the Lord in humility, poverty, and simplicity of heart.[50]

Francis is persecuted by the townspeople and his family.

At the same time, many mocked him, believing he had lost his mind. On the other hand, there were others who were moved to tears; they saw how this young man had passed so quickly from a life of pleasure and whims to an existence transfigured by the intoxication of divine love. But Francis paid no attention to any mockery and fervently gave thanks to God. It would be long and difficult to narrate just how much he suffered

---

50 *Anonymous of Perugia*, 1495.

in restoring [those churches]. Accustomed as he once was to every luxury in his father's house, behold, now he carries stones on his shoulders and suffers many sacrifices to serve God.[51]

When his father saw him persevering in good works, since he considered serving Christ to be folly, he began to persecute him and torment him, whenever he came across him, with curses. Then the servant of God called a very simple man of humble condition and begged him to take the place of his father. When his [father] multiplied his curses, [the poor man] would bless Francis in return. Thus, he translated into practice and demonstrated with deeds the meaning of the words of the Psalmist, "Though they curse, may you bless" (Ps 108(109):28).[52]

One winter morning, while vested in miserable clothes, Francis was insistent on praying. His brother passed by and said ironically to a fellow citizen, "Tell Francis to sell you a penny of his sweat!" Upon hearing those mocking words, the man of God was inundated with superhuman joy and replied in French, "I will sell this sweat, and very dearly, to my Lord."[53]

---

51 *Legend of the Three Companions*, 1421.

52 Celano, *Second Life*, 596.

53 *Legend of the Three Companions*, 1424.

One day, Francis was going through the streets of Assisi begging for oil for the lamps of San Damiano, the church he was then repairing. Upon entering a certain house, he saw a group of [his former] companions in front of the door and withdrew, red with shame. But he turned his noble spirit to Heaven and reproached himself for such cowardice, becoming a stern judge of himself. He then returned immediately to the house and explained confidently to everyone the reason for his shame. Practically intoxicated in the spirit, he asked in French for the oil he needed, which he obtained.[54]

Francis prophesies the arrival of St. Clare and the Poor Ladies in San Damiano.

Persisting in the restoration work [of San Damiano] with other workers, Francis was filled with spiritual joy. He said aloud in French to the neighbors and to those who passed by the church, "Come, help me in the work for the church of San Damiano. For here, there will be a monastery of ladies, and through the fame of their holy life, our heavenly Father will be glorified throughout the Church." In this way, filled

---

54 Celano, *Second Life*, 599.

with a prophetic spirit, he foretold what would actually happen.[55]

For [San Damiano] is the blessed and holy place in which the glorious religion and most noble Order of "Poor Ladies" and holy virgins, almost six years after his conversion, had its happy origin, through the work of Francis himself. There, Lady Clare, also a native of Assisi, a most precious and strong stone, became the foundation stone for all the other stones placed upon it. She, in fact, had been won over to God by the encouraging admonitions of the saint. After the beginning of the Order of the Friars Minor, she became a cause of spiritual progress and an example for countless souls. She was noble by birth, more noble by grace; virgin in body, pure in spirit; young in age, mature in wisdom; constant in purpose, ardent with enthusiasm in the love of God; full of wisdom and singular humility. She was Clare by name, more clear by life, most clear in virtue.[56]

Aided by the devotion of the faithful, who had already begun to recognize in the man of God an extraordinary virtue, Francis restored not only San Damiano but also two other churches that were also crumbling

---

55 *Legend of the Three Companions*, 1426.

56 Celano, *First Life*, 351–352.

and abandoned. One was dedicated to the Prince of the Apostles [San Pietro in Spina], while the other [was dedicated] to the glorious Virgin [that is, Our Lady of the Angels, also known as the Portiuncula].[57]

Francis establishes his residence at St. Mary of the Angels.

When the man of God saw [the church of Our Lady of the Angels] so abandoned, driven by his fervent devotion to the Queen of the world, he began to assiduously reside in that place with the intention of repairing it. Hearing that there were frequent apparitions of angels there, as indicated by the name of the church itself, called since ancient times St. Mary of the Angels, he decided to remain there because of his veneration for angels and his preeminent love for the Mother of Christ. The saint loved this place more than all other places in the world. Here, in fact, he began in humility [that is, purification]; here he progressed in virtue [that is, illumination]; here he happily arrived at fulfillment [that is, perfection]. At the moment of death, he recommended this place to the friars as the place dearest to the Virgin.[58]

57 Bonaventure, *Minor Legend*, 1338.

58 Bonaventure, *Major Legend*, 1048.

The dress Francis wore in that period was similar to that of hermits: a leather belt, a staff in his hand, and sandals on his feet.[59]

Feast of St. Matthias, February 24, AD 1208

Francis receives his vocation to Gospel poverty.

[In the church of Our Lady of the Angels], while he was devoutly attending the Mass of the Apostles, he heard the Gospel passage recited in which Christ sends out his disciples to preach and gives them the form of evangelical life, "Take no gold, nor silver, nor copper in your belts, no bag for your journey, nor two tunics, nor sandals, nor a staff" (Mt. 10:9–10 [RSVCE]).[60]

After the Mass, he asked the priest to explain the passage to him. The priest commented on it point by point. When Francis heard that Christ's disciples must neither possess gold, silver, or money; nor carry a bag, bread, or a staff on the road; nor have sandals or two tunics, but should only preach the Kingdom of God and penance, he immediately exulted in the Holy Spirit and exclaimed, "This is what I want, this is what I ask for, this is what I long to do with all my heart!"

---

59 Celano, *First Life*, 355.

60 Bonaventure, *Major Legend*, 1051.

Full of joy, the holy father then hastened to carry out the salutary admonition. He did not tolerate any delay in faithfully putting into practice what he heard.[61]

He immediately took off his shoes, rid himself of his staff, and repudiated his purse and money. Content with just one tunic, he removed his [leather] belt and used a cord in its stead. He put all the energy of his heart into seeking how to realize the things he had [just] heard and make himself in all respects compliant with the rule of apostolic sanctity.[62]

For he had not been a deaf hearer of the Gospel, but committing to a praiseworthy memory all that he heard, he sought with all diligence to carry it out to the letter.[63]

From that moment, by divine incitement, the man of God dedicated himself to emulating evangelical perfection and to inviting all others to penance. His discourses were not vain or inviting of laughter but were filled with the power of the Holy Spirit. They penetrated the depths of the heart and caused great amazement in his listeners.[64]

---

61 Celano, *First Life*, 356.

62 Bonaventure, *Minor Legend*, 1339.

63 Celano, *First Life*, 355.

64 Bonaventure, *Major Legend*, 1052.

Francis announces peace.

As he himself later confided, he learned a greeting from divine revelation, "The Lord give you peace!" And so in each of his preachings, at the beginning of the sermon, he greeted the people with this message of peace. It was an extraordinary fact that is almost miraculous: before his conversion, there was a precursor in the announcement of peace, who frequently went through Assisi greeting people with the expression, "Peace and good! Peace and good!" The conviction then developed that, just as John the Forerunner withdrew as soon as Jesus began his mission, so too that man, as a second John, preceded Francis in the greeting of peace but disappeared after the arrival of the Saint. And behold, animated by the spirit of the prophets and following their language, the man of God Francis, immediately after this herald announced peace, preached salvation. And through his salutary admonitions, many, many people who had previously lived in discordance with Christ and far from salvation made covenants of alliance with true peace.[65]

---

65 *Legend of the Three Companions*, 1428.

Part II: The Order

Companions

In this way, since many began to recognize the truth through both the man of God's simple teaching and life, some began to feel spurred by his example to do penance and join him. Thus, they took the habit and [embraced] his way of life by leaving everything.[66]

April AD 1208

Bernard of Quintavalle becomes Francis's first follower.

The first of these was Bernard of holy memory. After considering Francis's perseverance and fervor in serving God, how he restored those ruined churches with great toil, and how he who had previously lived in comfort now led such a harsh existence, [Bernard] resolved in his heart to give all his possessions to the poor and to firmly unite himself to Francis's way of

66 Bonaventure, *Major Legend*, 1053.

life and mode of dress. Thus, he went secretly to the man of God one day, revealed his decision to him, and arranged with him to see him on a certain evening. Blessed Francis—who had no companions as of yet—gave thanks to God and was filled with joy, for he knew that Messer Bernard led an exemplary life.[67]

As it was, Bernard invited Francis to dine and overnight with him, which Saint Francis accepted. In this way, Messer Bernard set his heart to contemplate his sanctity. He had a bed prepared for him in his own room, in which a lamp burned continuously throughout the night. Saint Francis, in order to conceal his sanctity, immediately upon entering the room threw himself on the bed and pretended to be asleep. Likewise, Messer Bernard, after some time, lay down and began to snore loudly, as if he, too, were sleeping soundly. Then Saint Francis, believing Messer Bernard to be asleep, arose from his bed and fell into prayer. Raising his eyes and hands to Heaven, with the greatest devotion and fervor, he said, "My God, my God." Saying this and weeping bitterly, he remained in this way until morning, repeating constantly, "My God, my God," and nothing else. [. . .] Upon witnessing Saint

---

67 *Legend of the Three Companions*, 1430.

Francis's most devout acts by oil lamp and devoutly considering the words he was saying, [Bernard] was touched and inspired by the Holy Spirit to amend his life.[68]

When morning came, [Francis and Bernard] entered the church [of San Nicolò]. After devout prayer, they opened the Gospel, ready to carry out the first counsel that was offered to them. After opening the book, Christ manifested his counsel with these words: "If you wish to be perfect, go, sell what you have and give to the poor, and you will have treasure in heaven. Then come, follow me" (Mt 19:21). They repeated the gesture, and another passage was revealed: "Take nothing for the journey" (Lk 9:3). They did so a third time and read, "If anyone wishes to come after me, he must deny himself and take up his cross daily and follow me" (Lk 9:23).[69]

Upon hearing these words, they were filled with great joy. [Editor: Some of the legends place Peter of Catanii together with Bernard and Francis]. Then they said, "This is what we desired; this is what we sought!" And blessed Francis said, "This will be our Rule."

---

68 *The Little Flowers*, 1827.

69 Celano, *Second Life*, 601.

Turning to the two, he added, "Go and put into practice the counsel you have heard from the Lord."[70]

Messer Bernard, who was very rich, went and sold all his possessions, obtaining a lot of money, which he distributed entirely to the poor of the city. Peter also carried out the divine counsel as best he could. Having stripped themselves of everything, they both put on the habit that the Saint had taken a short while earlier, after [Francis] abandoned [the tunic] of a hermit. Then, from that hour, they lived with him according to the form of the holy Gospel, as the Lord had indicated to them. Thus, Francis was able to write in his *Testament*, "The Lord himself revealed to me that I was to live according to the form of the holy Gospel."[71]

The requirements for following Francis are established.

Francis's conversion to God served as a model for all who came after him: they had to sell their possessions and distribute the proceeds to the poor. The arrival and conversion of such pious [men] filled Francis with extraordinary joy. It seemed to him that the Lord was

70 *Anonymous of Perugia*, 1497.

71 *Legend of the Three Companions*, 1423.

caring for him, giving him the companionship and faithful friends that everyone needs.[72]

The man of God Francis and the two brothers we have spoken of, as they did not have a place to live together, took refuge in a poor and abandoned church, known as St. Mary of the Portiuncula [also known as St. Mary of the Angels]. There they prepared a hut in which they lived together in community.[73]

April 23, AD 1208

A fourth companion arrives.

After eight days, a man from Assisi named Giles arrived. Full of faith and devotion, the Lord had granted him singular graces. With great devotion and reverence, he knelt down and requested that Francis receive him into his group. Delighted to see him, and upon hearing his request, the Saint welcomed him gladly. All felt pervaded by extraordinary spiritual joy.[74]

The saintly father Giles was truly filled with God and worthy of solemn remembrance. For he later became renowned for his sublime virtues, as the servant

72 Celano, *First Life*, 361.

73 *Legend of the Three Companions*, 1435.

74 *Anonymous of Perugia*, 1502.

of the Lord had prophesied of him. And although he was illiterate and simple, he rose to the highest peaks of contemplation. For long periods of time, Giles devoted himself incessantly to mystical ascents. He was raptured in God with such frequent ecstasies that even though he was among men, he seemed to be leading a life more angelic than human. I [St. Bonaventure] have witnessed this with my own eyes, and I bear witness to it.[75]

Spring AD 1208

The first four depart on the first mission.

The four gathered together, overflowing with indescribable joy and happiness in the Holy Spirit. In view of greater spiritual profit, they divided themselves as follows: Francis and Giles went to the March of Ancona, while the other two set out for another region. While going toward that region, [Francis and Giles] rejoiced joyfully in the Lord. In a loud and clear voice, Francis sang the praises of the Lord in French, blessing and glorifying the goodness of the Most High. Such was their joy that it seemed they had discovered a

75 Bonaventure, *Major Legend,* 1055.

magnificent treasure in the evangelical garden of Lady Poverty, for the love of which they had generously and spontaneously rid themselves of all material possessions, considering all as rubbish.[76]

Francis was not yet preaching to the people of God. But while he passed through cities and castle settlements, he exhorted men and women to fear and love the Creator of Heaven and earth and to do penance for their sins. Giles limited himself to saying, "What he says is very good. Believe him." Their listeners asked themselves, "Who are these two, and what are they saying?" Some responded that they were fanatics or drunkards. Others, on the contrary, maintained that what they were saying was not the talk of madmen. Another observed, "For thirst of supreme perfection, they follow the Lord and have lost their minds. Do you not see the desperate lives they lead? They go barefoot, dressed in despicable clothes, and they eat almost nothing." No one followed them. Moreover, women and girls, upon seeing them from afar, fled from them as if from fools. But although no one followed them, all were edified at the sight of their holy conduct. After

76 *Legend of the Three Companions*, 1435–1436.

having traveled through that region, they returned to the said place of St. Mary of the Angels.[77]

The first priest arrives.

[When Francis and the first companions had been giving away their goods,] a priest named Sylvester came. Blessed Francis had purchased some stones from him to restore the church of San Damiano, where he lived before he had companions. Seeing so much money being given away, that priest burned with impatient avarice and longed to obtain a handful himself. So he protested, saying, "Francis, you have not paid me in full for the stones I gave you." Hearing that unjust rebuke, the Saint, who was free from all avarice, approached Brother Bernard and, putting his hand in his cloak where the coins were, took out a handful of coins and offered them to the priest. He even took a second handful and poured them out to Sylvester, saying, "Is the debt fully paid?"

"Perfectly," Sylvester replied, and he went home exulting.

A few days later, Sylvester was inspired by the Lord. Reflecting on the gesture of blessed Francis, he said,

77 *Anonymous of Perugia*, 1504–1505.

"Truly, I am a wretch! Old as I am, here I am attached and furiously hunting for this [money], while that young man despises and abhors it for the love of God." [. . .] After a short time, he entered the Order, where he lived a holy life and died gloriously.[78]

Summer AD 1208

Then [there was] Brother Philip, whose lips the Lord had touched and purified with burning coal [see Is 6:5–7], so that he spoke of God with a wondrous spirit. He interpreted Scripture, explaining its most hidden meanings, without ever having studied. [79]

After a few days, three other men from Assisi arrived: Sabbatino, Morico, and John of la Capella. They beseeched Francis to receive them into the fraternity, and he welcomed them with humility and affection. When they went begging through the city, people would give them barely anything. Most of them would cover them with insults, "What! You have rid yourselves of your belongings, and now you want to eat at the expense of others?" Thus, they were forced to suffer a regrettable shortage. For their part, their parents

78 *Anonymous of Perugia*, 1499–1500.

79 Celano, *First Life*, 362.

and blood relatives could not stand them, and other citizens mocked them as eccentric, brainless people. In those days, in fact, no one dared to abandon their possessions and go from door to door asking for charity.[80]

80 *Legend of the Three Companions*, 1438.

Announcing the Gospel

Francis sends the brothers on mission a second time.

Then the pious father gathered all his children around him and spoke to them at length about the Kingdom of God, contempt for the world, and the necessity of denying one's own will and mortifying one's body. Then he revealed his intention to send them to the four parts of the world. By now the holy father, like the sterile, simple, and poor woman of the Bible, had given birth seven times and desired to give birth to all the faithful people for Christ, calling them to weeping and penance. [Editor: At this point, according to Bonaventure, Francis had seven followers.]

"Go," said the sweet father to his children, "and announce peace to men and preach penance for the remission of sins. Be patient in tribulations, vigilant in prayer, valiant in labors, modest in speech, coherent in behavior, and grateful for benefits received. And in compensation for all this, an eternal Kingdom has been prepared for you."[81]

Francis continued. "Do not be afraid of being considered insignificant or unbalanced, but proclaim penance with courage and simplicity. Have faith in the Lord, who has conquered the world! He speaks with his Spirit in you and through you, admonishing men and women to convert to him and observe his precepts. You will meet some faithful, meek, and benevolent [people], who will receive you and your words with joy. Many more, however, will be the unbelievers, the proud, and blasphemers, who will insult you and resist you and your message. Resolve, therefore, to bear everything with patience and humility."

Hearing the exhortation, the brothers became afraid. But the Saint continued, "Do not be afraid, because in a short time, many learned and noble people will come to us. They will join us in preaching to kings, princes, and many people. They will convert to the Lord in great numbers, and he will multiply and increase his family throughout the world."[82]

---

81 Bonaventure, *Major Legend*, 1058–1059.

82 *Legend of the Three Companions*, 1440.

Autumn AD 1208

Then Brother Bernard and Brother Giles left for Compostela—to the sanctuary of Saint James in Galicia, Spain. Saint Francis chose the valley of Rieti with another companion. The other four, two by two, set off in the other two directions.[83]

Their pious father and pastor went out to a solitary place [near the city of Poggio Bustone]. There, he wept in great bitterness of heart over his [former] life as a young man, which had been lived in guilt. While he asked for forgiveness and graces for himself and his followers, whom he had generated in Christ, he felt invaded by a singular, exuberant joy, and he felt assured that all his sins had been fully forgiven. Raptured and totally absorbed in a vivifying light, he saw luminously future events that concerned him and his brothers. For the comfort of his little flock, he later revealed these things in a familiar way when he foretold that through the clemency of God, the Order would progress and expand.[84]

During the journey, whenever the devout servants of the Lord came across a church that was consecrated

---

83 Celano, *First Life*, 368.

84 Bonaventure, *Minor Legend*, 1341.

or abandoned or a cross along the road, they stopped to recite this prayer with fervor, "We adore you, Lord Jesus Christ, here and in all your churches in the whole world, and we bless you, because by your holy cross you have redeemed the world." There they believed and felt the presence of the Lord.

Whoever saw them was amazed, saying, "Never have we seen religious dressed in this way." Being unlike all the others in dress and life, they seemed like woodland men. Upon entering a city, a castle settlement, or a house, they announced peace. Wherever they met men and women, whether on the street or in the squares, they admonished them to fear and love the Creator of Heaven and earth, to remember God's commandments that had fallen into oblivion, and to commit themselves to putting them into practice. There were those who listened to them with compassion and joy, and there were those who ridiculed them. Many bombarded them with questions, such that it was hard to shield themselves from so many interrogations. When there is something new, curiosity naturally arises. They would say, "Where are you from?" or "What order do you belong to?" But they would simply answer, "We are penitents, and we come from the city of Assisi." In fact, the friars' religion [that is, the movement] was not yet called an order.[85]

Francis and the friars experience persecutions.

Many took them for charlatans or simpletons and did not want to receive them in their homes for fear they were thieves. In various places, after having received many insults, they found no place to take refuge, except under the porticoes of churches or houses.[86]

Others treated them with contempt. People of high and modest status alike mocked and mistreated them, to the point of stripping them of their poor garments. The servants of God remained naked because, according to the evangelical ideal, they brought with them only one garment, and moreover, they did not ask for the return of what had been taken from them. However, if the embezzlers, moved by compassion, spontaneously decided to give their habits back to them, they received them quite willingly. Some threw mud at them, while others put dice in their hands, inviting them to play. Still others grabbed them from behind by the hood and dragged them on their backs. These and

85 *Anonymous of Perugia*, 1509.

86 *Legend of the Three Companions*, 1442.

other similar cruelties were inflicted on them because they were considered such low beings that they could be abused at will. Along with hunger and thirst, cold and nakedness, they suffered tribulations and sufferings of every kind.

But they bore everything with imperturbable patience, according to the admonition of Francis, without being overcome by sadness or hurt by resentment and without speaking ill of those who afflicted them. On the contrary, as perfect evangelical men, given the opportunity to realize great spiritual gains, they rejoiced in the Lord, considering it a blessing to be exposed to such trials and hardships. Faithful to the word of the Gospel, they prayed solicitously and fervently for their persecutors.[87]

The friars return to Assisi.

Early AD 1209

Shortly after that departure, the good father felt a great desire to see his dear children again, and since he could not bring them back himself, he prayed that the One who gathers the dispersed of Israel would do so

87 *Legend of the Three Companions*, 1444.

now. So it happened that without the need for human prompting, unexpectedly and wondrously, they all found themselves together, according to his desire and by the work of divine goodness. Then, four more good men joined them, so that they reached the number twelve.[88]

Only the bishop of Assisi, to whom the man of God often turned for advice, received [Francis] with benevolence. He once said to Francis, "Your life seems harsh to me, since you possess nothing in this world." But the saint replied, "Messer, if we had goods, we would also have to have weapons to defend them. From wealth arise disputes and quarrels, and thus hinders the love of God and neighbor in many ways. For this reason, we do not want to possess any material goods in this world." The bishop was pleased with the response of the man of God, who despised all transitory riches, especially money.[89]

---

88 Bonaventure, *Major Legend*, 1060.

89 *Legend of the Three Companions*, 1438.

Papal Approval

Francis writes a Rule and goes to Rome, seeking approval from the pope.

Francis wrote several Rules, which he tested before composing the definitive one, which he left to his brothers.[90]

Spring AD 1209

With that, the servant of the Lord decided to present himself to the Apostolic See with his gaggle of simple men to ask humbly and insistently the most Holy See to confirm with its plenary authority the *Rule of Life* that the Lord had previously shown him and that he had also written in brief words.[91]

---

90 *Legend of the Three Companions*, 1439.

91 Bonaventure, *Minor Legend*, 1341.

So, with those aforementioned [eleven friars, he went to Rome, greatly desiring that the Lord Pope confirm what he had written. [. . .] At that time, Pope Innocent III was in charge of the Church of God. He was covered with glory in learning, rich in eloquence, and a fervent cultivator of justice in defending the rights and interests of the Christian faith.[92]

[Along the way,] God looked down upon the desire of his servant and sent [Francis] the following vision to strengthen the courage of his companions, who were terrified by the awareness of their own simplicity. It seemed to [Francis] that he was walking on a road, beside which stood a very tall tree. Upon approaching the tree, he began to observe its height from below, when suddenly a divine force lifted him up so high that he was able to touch the top of the tree and bend its top to the ground with extreme ease. The man of God understood perfectly that this vision was a presage and was indicating to him how the apostolic authority [that is, the pope] in his condescension [that is, lowering himself] would bend down to him. With his soul filled with joy, he comforted his companions and faced the journey with them.[93]

---

92 Celano, *First Life*, 373–375.

93 Bonaventure, *Major Legend*, 1061.

While they were on their way, Francis said, "Let us make one of us our guide and consider him as the vicar of Jesus Christ. Wherever he goes, let us follow him, and when he wants to stop, let us stop." They chose Brother Bernard, the first disciple of Francis, and did what he said. They went about joyfully, talking about the words of the Lord. Nothing came out of their mouths except what was for the praise and glory of the Lord and the profit of their souls; otherwise, they prayed. And the Lord provided them with food and lodging in due time.[94]

When they arrived in Rome, they met the bishop of Assisi, who received them with great joy. He had great respect for Francis and all the brothers. [. . .] The bishop of Assisi was a friend of Cardinal John of St. Paul, bishop of Sabina, a man truly full of the grace of God and particularly drawn to men of holy life. Having learned from the bishop of Assisi of the story of Francis and his brothers, John greatly desired to meet the Saint and some of his companions. [. . .] In the few days that [the friars] spent with him, they edified [the cardinal] with their holy discourse and example. The cardinal, realizing that the information he had received

---

94 *Anonymous of Perugia*, 1523.

was true, humbly and devoutly recommended himself to their prayers and asked as a special favor to be considered one of them.

Then he questioned Francis about the reason for his coming. When he learned of the purpose, which was dear to him, he offered to represent them to the Roman Curia. [The cardinal] then went there and said to the Lord Pope Innocent III, "I have met a man of extraordinary virtue who has committed to living the evangelical ideal, observing in all things the perfection expressed in the Gospel. I am convinced that the Lord wants, through him, to reform the faith of the Holy Church throughout the world." These words greatly impressed the Pope, who ordered the cardinal to bring Francis to him.[95]

Francis, therefore, hastened to present himself, as arranged, before the Supreme Pontiff, Pope Innocent III. Christ, through the power and wisdom of God, had come to [the pope] earlier: in his condescension and clemency, through a vision, [Christ] admonished his Vicar to listen with gentleness and to consent with benevolence to the supplications of that poor man. In fact, the Roman Pontiff had a dream in which the

---

95 *Legend of the Three Companions*, 1456–1457.

Lateran Basilica was about to collapse. However, a poor, small, and despicable man was supporting it with his shoulders so that it would not fall. The wise pontiff, upon contemplating in the servant of God his poverty and constancy in pursuing perfection, zeal for souls, and burning fervor of holy will, exclaimed, "Truly this is the one who will uphold the Church of Christ through his works and teachings."[96]

[Editor: in a later edition, the following passage was added by the successor of St. Bonaventure.] When Francis arrived at the Roman Curia, he was led into the presence of the Supreme Pontiff. The Vicar of Christ, however, was walking in the Lateran Palace in the place called the Speculum. Immersed in deep thought, he indignantly chased away the servant of Christ as an importunate person, and Francis left humbly. The following night, however, the Pontiff had a revelation from God. He saw at his feet a palm tree that was growing little by little until it became a beautiful tree. While the Vicar of Christ wondered in amazement what this vision meant, the divine light impressed on his mind the idea that the palm tree represented the poor man whom he had chased away a day earlier. The next

96 Bonaventure, *Minor Legend*, 1342.

morning, the Pope had his servants search the city for the poor man. They found him in the hospital of St. Anthony near the Lateran, and for the Pope's convenience, they immediately brought him to him.[97]

Having presented himself to the Roman Curia and being brought before the Supreme Pontiff, [Francis] explained his intentions and humbly and earnestly asked him to approve the *Rule of Life* he had written. The Vicar of Christ, Pope Innocent III, truly illustrious for wisdom, admiring the man of God's purity and simplicity of soul, firmness of purpose, and fiery ardor of holy will, felt inclined to accept his requests with pious assent. However, he did not want to approve the *Rule of Life* proposed by the poor man immediately because, to some cardinals, it seemed strange and beyond human strength.

Cardinal John of St. Paul—the Bishop of Sabina, a venerable man, lover of all sanctity, and supporter of the poor man of Christ—was inflamed by the Spirit of God. He said to the Supreme Pontiff and his brother cardinals, "This poor man, in reality, asks us only that a form of evangelical life be approved for him. If, therefore, we reject his request as being too difficult and

---

97 Bonaventure, *Major Legend*, 1063.

strange, let us be careful that we do not injure the Gospel. For if anyone were to say that in observing evangelical perfection and in vowing to practice it there is something strange, irrational, or impossible, he would be guilty of blasphemy against Christ, the author of the Gospel."[98]

The Pope, thus, wanted to be certain that the approval granted and the favors he promised corresponded to the will of the Lord. Therefore, before taking leave of the Saint, he said to him and his companions, "Dear children, your way of life seems too hard and difficult to Us. [Editor: the pontiff is using the royal we.] However, since your fervor is so sincere, it is not possible for Us to doubt you. Nonetheless, it is Our duty to be concerned with those who will be your followers in the future, so that they do not find your path too arduous."

Instead, he observed that their faith was so firm and their hope was so strongly anchored in Christ that they were not led to accept any mitigation of their generous impulse. So, he said to Francis, "Son, go and pray to God to reveal to you whether your request proceeds

---

98 Bonaventure, *Major Legend*, 1062.

from his will. When the will of the Lord is manifested to Us, We will come to meet your desires."[99]

The Saint obeyed the command of the Supreme Pastor and [went away and] turned to Christ with complete confidence. He prayed insistently and also exhorted his companions to devoutly supplicate God. In short, while he was praying, he received a salutary answer, which he communicated to his sons, who came to know that Christ had spoken to him the following parable, which he would say to the Pope:

There lived in a desert a poor but very beautiful woman. A king fell in love with her because of her enchanting appearance, joyfully entered into a relationship with her, and begat very beautiful children. When they were adults and nobly educated, the mother said to them, "Do not be ashamed, my beloved, at being poor, because you are all children of that great king. Therefore, go joyfully to his court and ask him for what you need." Marveling and delighted at these words and animated by the assurance that they were of royal lineage and future heirs, they considered their extreme poverty to be wealth, and they presented themselves to the king with confidence and without fear because their visages

99 *Legend of the Three Companions*, 1458.

mirrored his visage. Seeing that they resembled him, the king was amazed and asked whose children they were. When they answered that they were children of that poor and lonely woman in the desert, he embraced them, saying, "You are my children and heirs. Do not be afraid. Because if strangers are fed at my table, it is certainly more just that those who have the right to the entire inheritance should be fed." He then ordered the woman to send all the children he had fathered to his court so that they could be raised there.[100]

The man of God, Francis, immediately understood that this poor woman represented him. This rendered his resolution to observe most holy poverty even stronger in the future. Having risen, he went immediately to the Apostolic See to explain to the Pope what the Lord had revealed to him.[101]

[The Saint then recounted to the pope] in detail the parable revealed to him by the Lord. He added, "Lord, I am that poor woman whom God loves and, in his mercy, has made beautiful and from whom he was pleased to beget children. The King of kings has promised me that he will raise all the children he has had by me, because if he feeds strangers, how much more will

---

100 Celano, *Second Life*, 602–603.

101 *Anonymous of Perugia*, 1527–1528.

he care for his own children? That is, if God lavishes temporal goods on sinners and the unworthy, moved by love for his creatures, all the more will he be generous with evangelical men, who are deserving of them."

This reasoning struck the Pope deeply, especially because, before the arrival of Francis, he too had had a strange vision [of the Lateran Basilica falling down]. The pontiff, considering his fervor in the service of God and comparing his vision with the symbolic story related to him by Francis, concluded, "Truly, this is the religious and holy man through whom the Church of God will be raised up and supported." He embraced the Saint and approved his Rule. He also authorized him and his companions to preach penance everywhere, with the condition that the friars also have permission to preach from Francis. In consistory, the pontiff then confirmed the approval granted to the new movement.[102]

[After giving his assent, the pope] encouraged them with many counsels and blessed them, saying, "Go with God, brothers, and as he deigns to inspire you, preach penance to all. When the almighty Lord makes you grow in number and grace, happily return to recount

102 *Legend of the Three Companions*, 1460.

to Us, and We will more confidently grant you other favors and more important offices."[103]

Blessed Francis then bowed and promised the Lord Pope obedience and reverence with humility and devotion. In turn, the other brothers, who had not yet promised obedience, by order of the Pope, likewise promised obedience and reverence to Francis. And the Lord Pope approved the Rule for him and for his brothers present and future. He also gave him authority to preach everywhere, according to the grace given him by the Holy Spirit. He also authorized the other brothers to preach, to whom blessed Francis wished to grant the ministry of preaching.[104]

From that time on, [the pope] felt an extraordinary devotion to the servant of Christ and was inclined to accept [Francis's] requests in all respects, and he always loved him with special affection.[105]

---

103 Celano, *First Life*, 375.

104 *Anonymous of Perugia*, 1528.

105 Bonaventure, *Major Legend*, 1064.

Having received the blessing from Innocent III, Francis and his eleven companions went to visit the tombs of the Apostles. The Cardinal of St. Paul obtained the tonsure for them since he wanted all twelve to be added to the clergy.[106]

106 *Legend of the Three Companions*, 1461.

A New Pentecost

The friars return to Assisi enthusiastic to evangelize.

Then the man of God departed from Rome with his brothers, heading for the evangelization of the world. He was filled with wonder at seeing his desire realized so readily. Every day his hope and trust in the Savior—who had foretold everything to him with his holy revelations—grew.[107]

Relying on divine grace and papal authority, Francis was full of confidence. He headed towards the Spoleto Valley, ready to practice and teach the Gospel. Along the way, he discussed with his companions how to sincerely observe the Rule they had embraced, how to progress in all holiness and justice before God, and how to sanctify themselves and be examples to others. The conversation went on for a long time, and the day

107 *Legend of the Three Companions*, 1462.

passed. Tired and hungry from the toil, they stopped in an isolated place. But it was not possible to make provisions for even a little food anywhere. Then the Providence of God intervened without delay. Suddenly a man appeared with a loaf of bread in his hand, gave it to the poor men of Christ, and immediately disappeared. It was not known from whence he had come or where he was going. Then the poor friars recognized that the presence of this man of God was a guarantee of Heaven for them on their journey, and they felt satisfied more by the gift of divine generosity than by the nourishment that their bodies received. Moreover, filled with divine consolation, they firmly and irrevocably reaffirmed their commitment never to abandon, either through hunger or through tribulation, the holy poverty they professed.[108]

After having restored themselves with that food, they continued on to a place near Orte and stayed there for about fifteen days. Some of them went into the city to look for food and brought back to the others what they had managed to gather by begging from door to door. They ate it together joyfully and thanked the Lord. If there was anything left over, when they

108 Bonaventure, *Major Legend*, 1065.

could not give it to the poor, they put it in a pit, which had once served as a tomb, to eat the following day. That place was deserted, and almost no one passed by there.[109]

Francis and the brothers consider whether the Order should be contemplative or apostolic.

Francis then raised with his companions the question as to whether they should live habitually among the people or seclude themselves in solitary places. After having examined the divine will on this point through persistent prayer, he was enlightened by the response of a heavenly revelation. He understood that he had been sent by God for this purpose: to win for Christ souls that the devil tries to steal. He therefore established that one had to choose to live for all rather than for oneself alone.[110]

---

109 Celano, *First Life*, 378.

110 Bonaventure, *Minor Legend*, 1343.

Summer AD 1209

The friars settle in Rivotorto, in the plains near Assisi.

Back in Assisi, father [Francis] settled with his sons in a place near Assisi called Rivotorto, where there was a hovel abandoned by everyone. [Editor: *Rivotorto* means "crooked stream" in old Italian.] The hovel was so small that they could barely sit down or lie down. Often there was no bread, and they lived on turnips obtained as alms by begging here and there.[111]

Francis constantly sought holy simplicity, and he did not allow the narrowness of the place to impede the expansions of the spirit. Therefore, he wrote the names of the brothers on the beams of the hovel so that each would recognize his own place for prayer and rest, and the narrowness of the place would not disturb the recollection of their souls.[112]

They lived [in Rivotorto] by much toil and hardship according to the form of holy poverty and were concerned more with the refreshment of the bread of tears than with the bread of abundance. They were continually intent on praying to God and applying themselves to the exercise of prayer and devotion more with

111 *Legend of the Three Companions*, 1464.

112 Celano, *First Life*, 397.

the mind than with the voice. This is because they did not yet have liturgical books with which to recite the canonical hours. Instead of books, they read unceasingly, leafing through the book of the cross of Christ day and night, instructed by the example and word of father [Francis], who continually spoke to them about the cross of Christ. He taught them to praise God in all creatures and to take their cue from all creatures, to honor priests with special devotion, and to firmly believe and sincerely confess the truth of the faith as the holy Roman Church holds and teaches. In all things, they observed the teachings of the holy father.[113]

Francis's style of preaching deeply impacts the people.

They set out [from Rivotorto] to preach the word of God to the people, according to the opportunity of the time and place. Having become a herald of the Gospel, Francis went through the cities and towns, announcing the Kingdom of God not with the learned language of human wisdom but with the power of the Holy Spirit. The Lord directed him with anticipatory

---

113 Bonaventure, *Major Legend*, 1067; 1069.

revelations, and [God] confirmed his word with miracles that accompanied it.[114]

Since he had received permission from the Apostolic See, Francis acted confidently and securely, avoiding flattery and enticement. It was not his custom to allay vices but to scourge them firmly. He did not seek excuses for the lives of sinners but struck them with harsh rebukes, since he had first of all forced himself to do what he instructed in others. Thus, he did not fear that he would be found inconsistent, and he preached the truth with frankness, so that even the most learned and famous men received his inspired words with admiration, and in his presence, they were filled with a salutary fear.

Men and women, clerics and religious, all flocked to see and hear the holy one of God, who appeared to everyone as a man from another world. People of every age and sex were eager to admire the wonders that the Lord was once again accomplishing in the world through his servant. The presence or even the mere fame of Saint Francis seemed to be truly a new light sent from Heaven at that time to dispel the murky darkness that had invaded the earth, to the point that

---

114 Bonaventure, *Minor Legend*, 1343.

almost no one could discern the way to salvation. For practically everyone had fallen into such a profound forgetfulness of the Lord and his commandments that they could hardly bear to move a little from their hardened and inveterate vices.[115]

Francis appears to the friars in a spiritual vision.

Once, as was his custom, he was intent on keeping vigil in prayer, physically far from his children. About midnight, while some of the friars were sleeping and some were praying, a wondrously splendid chariot of fire, over which there was a globe comprised of very bright fire in the shape of the sun, entered through the little door of the friars' dwelling and turned back and forth three times through the house. At that wondrous and clear sight, those who were awake were astonished, and those who were asleep were awakened and terrified, and they all felt with equal intensity a clarity of the heart and of the body. By virtue of that wonderful light, the conscience of each brother was naked before the consciences of the others. Together, they all understood that the Lord had allowed them to see the holy father Francis transfigured in that image, which they

115 Celano, *First Life*, 382–383.

read in each other's hearts. It signified that he had come in the spirit and power of Elijah and had been elected prince of the spiritual militia, chariot of Israel, and its charioteer. Indeed, after the Saint returned among the friars, he began to strengthen them spiritually. On the basis of the vision shown to them from Heaven, he began to closely scrutinize the secrets of their consciences and to predict, moreover, the future, and to shine with such miracles as to show clearly and manifestly how the double spirit of Elijah had rested upon him with its fullness: that following [Francis's] teaching and [form of] life was the surest thing for all.[116]

September AD 1209

Otto IV travels through the Spoleto Valley to be crowned emperor by the pope.

When one day Emperor Otto was passing through those regions with great pomp and fanfare, on his way to receive the crown of the earth, the most holy father [Francis] would not even leave his hovel, which was near the route of transit. Nor did he allow his followers to go there, except one who was to announce firmly to

---

116 Bonaventure, *Minor Legend*, 1344.

the emperor that his glory would last but a short while. Since the glorious Saint had his home in the depths of his heart, where he prepared a worthy dwelling place for God, the external world with its din could never distract him, nor could any voice interrupt the great work on which he was intent. He felt himself invested with apostolic authority, and therefore, he firmly refused to flatter kings and princes.[117]

Late AD 1209 or early AD 1210.

The friars leave Rivotorto for St. Mary of the Angels.

One day, while the friars were there [in Rivotorto], a peasant arrived, followed by his donkey, intending to enter the hovel with the animal. So that the friars would not resist, the peasant leaned out and said to the donkey, "Come in, come in, for we will do good to this place." The holy father, upon hearing these words and understanding the peasant's intention, felt a surge of hostility toward the importunate person, especially because he had made such a great racket with his donkey, disturbing the brothers, who at that moment were immersed in silence and prayer. But Francis said

117 Celano, *First Life*, 396.

to them, "I see, brothers, that God has not called us to prepare a stable for the donkey, nor to have trouble with people, but to go and preach to men the way of salvation through good counsel and even more by devoting ourselves to prayer and thanksgiving." So they left that hovel used by poor lepers, and they moved to St. Mary of the Angels [also known as the Portiuncula], next to which there was a small house, where they had lived before obtaining that church.

Subsequently, following the will and inspiration of God, Francis humbly requested [usage of] the church from the [Benedictine] abbot of San Benedetto of Monte Subasio, near Assisi. And he [later] recommended it with affectionate insistence to the minister general and to all the brothers as the favorite place of the glorious Virgin among all the churches of the world.[118]

Although the abbot and monks had granted the church as a gift to blessed Francis and his brothers without wanting any return or annual tribute, nevertheless blessed Francis, as a skilled and experienced master who intended to found his house on the solid rock, that is, to found his group on true poverty, sent

---

118 *Legend of the Three Companions*, 1465.

a basket full of small fish called graylings annually to the monastery. This was a sign of sincere humility and poverty, so that the brothers would not own any place, nor even live there, unless it was under the dominion of others, so that they would not have the power to sell or alienate it in any way. Every year, when the brothers brought the little fish to the monks, in grace of the humility of blessed Francis, [the monks] gave him and his brothers a jar full of oil.[119]

---

119 *Legend of Perugia/Assisi Compilation*, 1552.

The Order of Friars Minor

It is now time to focus our attention on the Order that Francis raised up by his love and brought to life by his profession. For he himself founded the Order of Friars Minor, and this is the occasion on which he gave it that name. [Editor: The Latin name, *Ordo Fratrum Minorum*, means Order of Lesser Brothers.] When those words were written in the Rule, "Let them be minors," as soon as he heard them, he exclaimed, "I want this Fraternity to be called the Order of Friars Minor." And they were truly "lesser," "subject to all," and they sought the lowest places and offices that were associated with humiliation in order to lay a solid foundation of true humility, on which the spiritual edifice of all the virtues could be built.[120]

On another occasion, blessed Francis said, "The Order and life of the Friars Minor can be compared to

120 Celano, *First Life*, 386.

a small flock that the Son of God, in these end times, asked of his heavenly Father, saying, 'Father, I would like you to create and give me a new and humble people in this final hour—people who would be different in humility and poverty from all others who preceded them and would be content to possess only me.' The Father answered his beloved Son, 'My Son, what you have asked is granted to you.'"[121]

Francis loved the Portiuncula more than any other place.

In this place [St. Mary of the Angels], there stood a church dedicated to the Virgin Mother, who, for her particular humility, after her Son, deserved to be head of all the Saints. Here the Order of Minors began, and their noble construction rose large and harmonious, as if resting on a solid foundation. The Saint loved this place more than any other and commanded the friars to venerate it with particular devotion. He wanted it to always be guarded as a mirror of the Order in humility and utmost poverty, with its ownership maintained by others, retaining only its use for himself and his sons.[122]

---

121 *Mirror of Perfection*, 1710.

122 Celano, *Second Life*, 604.

For this reason, he used to say to the brothers, "Be careful, my sons, never to abandon this place! If they drive you away in one direction, return to it in the other, because this place is holy. It is the dwelling place of Christ and of the Virgin, his mother.[123]

Francis surrounded the Mother of Jesus with an indescribable love because she made the Lord of majesty our brother. He sang special praises in her honor, he lifted up prayers, and he offered so many and such affections that the human language cannot express. But what fills us most with joy is that he made her Advocate of the Order and placed under her wings the children he was about to leave, so that they would find warmth and protection until the end.[124]

Francis shone like a bright star in the darkness of the night, and like morning light, he spread over the darkness. Thus, in a short time the appearance of the entire region changed. Losing its horror, it became more cheerful. The long drought was over. In the previously squalid fields, the harvest grew abundantly. By the grace of the Lord, even the uncultivated vineyard began to be covered with fragrant flowers and to ripen in sweet fruits of goodness and bounty. Thanksgiving

---

123 *Mirror of Perfection*, 1780.

124 Celano, *Second Life*, 786.

and hymns of praise resounded everywhere, and not a few, leaving worldly cares, following the example and teaching of Saint Francis, learned to know, love, and respect their Creator.[125]

Francis inspires the beginning of the Second and Third Orders.

Many noblemen and commoners, clerics and laity, who were docile to divine inspiration, went to the Saint, eager to join forever with him and under his guidance. As a rich source of heavenly grace, he gives to all the life-giving waters that make virtues bloom in the garden of the heart. He is truly a glorious artist and teacher of the evangelical life. Through his example, Rule, and teaching, the Church of Christ is renewed in its faithful men and women, and the threefold militia of the elect triumphs. To everyone he gave a Rule of Life and showed the way of salvation to each according to his or her condition.[126]

It was not only men who converted by entering the Order, but also many virgins and widows. Touched by the preaching of the friars and following their counsel,

---

125 Celano, *First Life*, 384–385.

126 Celano, *First Life*, 384–385.

they locked themselves away in the monasteries of their cities and towns to do penance. A friar was chosen with the task of being their visitor and director.[127]

March 18–19, AD 1212

On Palm Sunday, 1212, St. Clare leaves her home to become the first female follower of Francis and foundress of the Order of Poor Clares, historically known as the Second Order.

Among them, Clare, a virgin most dear to God, was the first little plant, and she exhaled her perfume like a white spring flower and shone like a most brilliant star. Now glorious in Heaven, she is rightly venerated on earth by the Church—she who was, in Christ, the daughter of the poor father Saint Francis and the mother of the Poor Ladies.[128]

St. Francis conceives a Third Order for laity.

Going with impetuosity of spirit without considering the way or the place, [the friars] came to a castle settlement called Savurniano, where Saint Francis

127 *Legend of the Three Companions*, 1472.

128 Bonaventure, *Major Legend*, 1074.

began to preach. [. . .] He preached with such fervor that all the men and women of that castle settlement, out of devotion, wanted to follow him and abandon the settlement. But Saint Francis did not permit them, saying to them, "Do not hurry and do not leave, and I will order what you must do for the salvation of your souls." Then he thought of creating the Third Order for the universal salvation of all. And so, leaving them quite consoled and well-disposed to penance, he departed from there.[129]

Even married men and women, unable to free themselves from the bonds of marriage, at the suggestion of the friars, practiced stricter penance in their homes. Thus, through Francis, the perfect worshipper of the Trinity, the Church of God was renewed by these three Orders, as had been prefigured by the restoration of the three churches carried out by the Saint. Each of these three Orders was approved, in its own time, by the Supreme Pontiff. [Editor: Originally known as the Order of Penitents, the Franciscan lay Order became known as the Third Order, while today it is known as the Secular Franciscan Order.][130]

---

129 *The Little Flowers*, 1846.

130 *Legend of the Three Companions*, 1472.

AD 1209–1210

Francis writes a letter to the Brothers and Sisters of Penance, considered the beginning of his guidance of the Third Order.

All who love the Lord with their whole heart, with their whole soul and mind, with all their strength, and love their neighbors as themselves and hate their bodies with their vices and sins, and receive the Body and Blood of our Lord Jesus Christ, and produce worthy fruits of penance—oh, how happy and blessed are these men and women when they do these things and persevere in doing them, because "the spirit of the Lord will rest upon them" (see Is. 11:2, translated from the original text) and will make "his home and dwelling among them" (see Jn 14:23, translated from the original text). And they are the sons of the heavenly Father, whose works they do; and they are the spouses, brothers, and mothers of our Lord Jesus Christ; we are spouses when, by the Holy Spirit, the faithful soul is united with our Lord Jesus Christ; we are brothers to him when we fulfill "the will of the Father who is in Heaven" (see Mt 7:21, translated from the original text); we are mothers when we carry him in our heart and body through divine love and a pure and sincere conscience; we give birth to him through a holy life, which must give light to others by example. Oh, how glorious it is to have a great and holy Father in Heaven! Oh, how glorious it is to have such a beautiful and admirable Spouse, the Holy Paraclete. Oh, how glorious it is to have such a Brother and such a Son—loved, beloved, humble, peaceful, sweet, lovable, and desirable above all. Our Lord Jesus Christ, who gave up his life for his sheep, prayed to the Father, saying, "Oh holy Father, protect them with your name, whom you gave me out of the world. I entrusted to them the message you entrusted to me, and they received it. They have known that, in truth, I came from you; they have believed that it was you who sent me. For these I pray, not for the world. Bless and consecrate them, and I consecrate myself for their sakes. I do not pray for them alone; I pray also for those who will believe in me through their word that they may be holy by being one as we are. And I desire, Father, to have them in my company where I am to see this glory of mine in your kingdom (see Jn 17:11, 8–9, 17, 19–21, 24, translated from the original text).[131]

---

131 St. Francis of Assisi, *Earlier Exhortation to the Brothers and Sisters of Penance*, 178.

Part III: Growth

The Form of Life

AD 1216

Jacques de Vitry, a French historian, prelate, and supporter of poverty movements throughout Europe, describes the early Franciscan movement.

After I frequented the Curia [for the funeral of Pope Innocent III in Perugia] for some time, I found many things there contrary to my spirit. All [the clergy and prelates] were so preoccupied with temporal and worldly things, matters of kings and kingdoms and litigation and trials that they hardly allowed any spiritual matters to be spoken of.

However, I discovered in those regions just one consolation to me: people of both sexes, wealthy and lay, were stripping themselves of all belongings for Christ and abandoning the world. They called themselves Friars Minor and Sisters Minor, and they are held in high esteem by the Pope and the cardinals. They do not meddle at all with temporal things. On the contrary, with fervent desire and vehement effort, they labor each day to snatch souls from worldly vanities who are about to shipwreck and draw them into their ranks. By divine grace, they have already produced great fruits, and many have made gains, so that those who listen to them invite others to come and see with their own eyes.

They live according to the form of the primitive Church, of which it is written that the community of believers was of one heart and one mind (see Acts 4:32). During the day, they enter the cities and towns, working actively to win others to the Lord. At night, they return to the hermitages or to some isolated place to devote themselves to contemplation. The women, on the other hand, live together in hospices not far from the cities and do not accept donations but live by the work of their own hands. They are greatly grieved and troubled in seeing themselves honored by clerics and laypersons more than they would like.[132]

A very strict discipline was observed in everything [at St. Mary of the Angels] in silence and at work, as well as in all the other aspects of the ruled life. No friar

---

132 Jacques de Vitry, Letter written from Genoa, 2202–2208.

could enter freely, except those expressly appointed. Gathered here from all parts, the Saint wanted them to be an example of devotion to God and perfect in everything. Access to any layperson was strictly forbidden. He did not want the small number of friars who lived here to be tickled by the itch of worldly news or be interrupted in their contemplation of heavenly goods to be dragged by chatterboxes to occupy themselves with earthly things. It was not permitted for anyone in this place to say idle words or to repeat those said by others. If someone happened to fail in this, he was warned never to repeat it again by a salutary punishment. The friars who lived there were busy day and night in divine praises, and they led an angelic life, fragrant with sweet perfume.[133]

Humility

Humility—the guardian and ornament of all the virtues—had by right taken possession of the man of God. In fact, although he shone with the privilege of many virtues, humility nevertheless seemed to have gained a special dominion over him, the least of all the

---

133 Celano, *Second Life*, 605.

Minors. And certainly, according to the criterion by which he judged himself, declaring himself the greatest sinner, a mere small and dirty vessel of clay; in reality, however, he was a chosen vessel of sanctity, shining and adorned with multiple virtues and grace, consecrated by purity.[134]

[Francis was] humble in demeanor, more humble in sentiment, most humble in his own esteem. By nothing could one distinguish that this prince of God had the office of superior, if not by this most shining gem, that he was the least among the lesser. This was the virtue, this was the title, and this was the badge that marked him as minister general. His mouth knew no haughtiness, his gestures no pomp, his acts no ostentation.[135]

The holy father did not want his brothers to be eager for knowledge and books; rather, he wanted and insisted that they strive to establish themselves on the foundation of holy humility and to follow pure simplicity, holy prayer, and lady poverty, which foundations the first holy brothers built upon. He said that [humility] alone was the sure way to one's own salvation and the edification of others, since Christ, whom

---

134 Bonaventure, *Minor Legend*, 1351.

135 Celano, *Second Life*, 724.

we are called to imitate, showed us and prescribed this ideal by word and example.[136]

From the beginning of his movement, he wanted the brothers to live in the leper hospitals to serve them and thus lay the foundation of humility. When they, noble or otherwise, entered the Order, among other things that were explained to them, it was said that it was necessary for them to serve the lepers and live in their houses.[137]

Francis used to say, "I want all my brothers to work and humbly practice honest work so that we are less of a burden to people and our hearts and tongues do not wander in idleness. Whoever does not know a trade, let him learn one." According to him, the recompense for work should not be available to the worker but to the guardian or the community.[138]

He venerated the prelates and priests of the Holy Church; he respected the lords, the nobility, and the rich; but he deeply loved the poor and shared tenderly in their sufferings. He showed himself to be the servant of all. Although he was above the entire fraternity, he designated one of those who lived with him as his

---

136 *Mirror of Perfection*, 1766.

137 *Mirror of Perfection*, 1730.

138 *Mirror of Perfection*, 1770.

guardian and master, and he obeyed him with humility and devotion in order to dispel every occasion of pride. He made himself small among men, bowing his head to the ground, in order to deserve, in the sight of God, to be exalted among the saints and the elect.[139]

Obedience

He tirelessly exhorted the brothers to faithfully observe the Gospel and the Rule, as they had promised, and especially to show themselves reverent and devoted to the liturgical offices and ecclesiastical ordinances, to listen fervently to the Mass, and to adore the Body of the Lord with utmost devotion. He wanted priests, who administer such venerable and sublime sacraments, to be especially honored: wherever [the friars] met them, they were to bow their heads before them and kiss their hands. If they saw them on horseback, [Francis] demanded that they kiss not only their hands but also the hooves of the horses on which they were riding out of reverence for the sacred powers with which God's ministers are invested.[140]

---

139 *Legend of the Three Companions*, 1467.

140 *Legend of the Three Companions*, 1468.

In order to fulfill all justice in the realization of perfect humility, Francis strove to remain subject not only to superiors but also to inferiors, to such an extent that he was accustomed to promising obedience even to the companion on a journey, even if the simplest friar. In this way, he did not command authoritatively, as in the manner of a prelate. Instead, in the manner of a minister and a servant, he obeyed even his subjects out of humility.[141]

He described the truly obedient [friar] as a dead corpse. He said, "Take a lifeless cadaver and place it where you like. You will see that it does not refuse if moved, does not murmur wherever it is assigned, and does not complain if it is transferred. If you place it on the chair, it will not look up but down. If it is placed in purple, it will seem doubly pale. Francis exclaimed, "This is the one who is truly obedient: the one who does not judge why he should be removed, does not care where he is assigned, and does not insist on being transferred. Raised to an office, he maintains the humility that is habitual to him. The more he is honored, the more unworthy he considers himself."[142]

---

141 Bonaventure, *Minor Legend*, 1351.

142 Celano, *Second Life*, 736.

Poverty and Simplicity

The first companions of Saint Francis strove with all their might to be poor in earthly things and rich in virtues, through which one attains true celestial and eternal riches.[143]

Holy poverty, which [the friars] carried with them as their only provision, made them ready for any obedience, robust for hard work, and ready for the journey. Since they had nothing earthly, they attached their hearts to nothing and feared losing nothing. They felt secure everywhere, untroubled by any care, not distracted by any preoccupation. With ease and without concerns, they looked forward to a refuge for the evening and the following day. [. . .] Scarcity itself was to them abundance and superabundance, while according to the counsel of the Master, they took pleasure not in greatness but in the smallest things.[144]

Francis preferred poverty to all perishable things as a pledge of an eternal inheritance. And he considered riches deceptive, as nothingness—a fiefdom granted for a moment. He loved poverty in preference to great riches and, in it, he desired to surpass all others—he

143 *The Little Flowers*, 1866.

144 Bonaventure, *Major Legend*, 1075.

who had learned from poverty to consider himself inferior to all.[145]

[The friars] were content with a single habit, sometimes patched inside and out. They were so poor and unrefined that in their way of dressing, they appeared truly crucified to the world. They tied the habit at the waist with a cord and wore rough trousers. Their holy purpose was to remain in that state without having anything else.[146]

In fact, from the beginning of his religious life until his death, [Francis] had as his wealth only a tunic, a cord, and trousers. He had nothing else. His poor appearance clearly indicated where he accumulated his wealth. For this reason, [he was] happy, confident, and agile in moving around. He enjoyed having exchanged the riches destined to perish for a good that was worth them one hundredfold.[147]

Through the love of highest poverty, the man of God became so flourishing and rich in holy simplicity that, although he had absolutely nothing of his own among the things of the world, he seemed to possess all good things since he possessed the very Author of

---

145 Bonaventure, *Minor Legend*, 1352.

146 Celano, *Second Life*, 388.

147 Celano, *Second Life*, 641.

this world. For with the acuity of the dove; that is, with the penetration that is proper to the simple mind, and with the pure gaze of reflection, he referred all things to the Supreme Artificer, and in all things he recognized, loved, and praised the Maker himself. And so it came to pass, by the gift of heavenly clemency, that he possessed all things in God and God in all things.[148]

[Holy simplicity] is that which places its glory in the fear of the Lord and which knows neither how to speak nor to do evil. It is the simplicity that examines itself and condemns no one in its judgment. It desires no ministry for itself but considers it due and awards it to the best. It is that which, not esteeming much the glories of Greece, prefers action to learning or teaching. It is the simplicity that in all divine laws leaves the tortuousness of words, ornaments, and tinsel, as well as the ostentation and curiosities to those who want to lose themselves. It seeks not the rind but the marrow, not the shell but the kernel, not many things but the more, supreme, and stable Good. This is the simplicity that father Francis required of the literate brothers and of those without culture alike. This is because he did not consider [simplicity] contrary to wisdom but,

148 Bonaventure, *Minor Legend*, 1353.

rightly, its sister, although he believed that those who are poor in knowledge can acquire and practice it more easily.[149]

Penance

They loved patience [that is, suffering] so much that they preferred to be where they had to suffer persecution rather than where, because their sanctity was known, they could enjoy the favors of the world. Often insulted, vilified, beaten, stripped, tied, and imprisoned, they endured everything virilely without seeking any defense. Indeed, their lips emitted only songs of praise and thanksgiving.[150]

When Francis lived at Our Lady of the Portiuncula and the friars were still few, he sometimes went to the villages and churches around Assisi, announcing and preaching to the people to do penance. During these trips, he carried a broom with which to clean the churches. For Francis suffered greatly when he entered a church and discovered it was dirty. Thus, after preaching to the people, he would have all the priests who were present gather in an out-of-the-way place so as

149 Celano, *Second Life*, 775.

150 Celano, *First Life*, 390.

not to be heard by the people. He spoke of the salvation of souls, but he especially instructed them to take the greatest care in keeping clean the churches, the altars, and all the furnishings used for the celebration of the divine mysteries.[151]

The brave soldier of Christ never had any regard for his body, which he exposed, as if it were not his own, to all the hardships of deed and of word. Anyone who wanted to detail what Francis suffered would go beyond the narration of the apostolic writings, in which the sufferings of the saints are told. In the same way, his first disciples, without exception, subjected themselves to all hardships, so that they considered it a sin to aspire to anything other than spiritual consolations.[152]

The illustrious follower of Jesus Crucified, the man of God Francis, from the beginning of his conversion, crucified the flesh and its passions with the rigor of discipline. Francis restrained the movements of the senses with the law of moderation in such a severe manner that he barely consumed sustenance [beyond what is] indispensable to nature. For his health, he rarely and with difficulty permitted himself cooked food. When he did, he sometimes made it bitter by mixing ashes

---

151 *Legend of Perugia/Assisi Compilation*, 1565.

152 Celano, *Second Life*, 607.

with it; otherwise, he rendered it tasteless by pouring water over it. He was severely sparing in drinking, and he kept his body from wine so that he might apply his mind to the light of wisdom. We see this clearly from this detail; that is, when he was tormented by the burning of thirst, he dared to barely drink even enough fresh water. Most often, the bare earth was the bed for his tired little body; a stone was his pillow; and a simple, wrinkled, and bristly garment was his blanket. He had learned from assured experience that malignant enemies are put to flight by hard and rough clothing; instead, they are encouraged by soft and delicate clothing to tempt with greater boldness.[153]

While they were severe with themselves, their behavior was always polite and peaceful with everyone else. They devoted themselves only to works of edification and peace, carefully avoiding every cause of bad example. They spoke only when necessary and never uttered incorrect or idle words. In all their lives and works, nothing could be found that was not honest and upright. Their bearing always shone with composure and modesty. They so mortified their senses that they saw and felt only what was essential and dutiful: their

153 Bonaventure, *Minor Legend*, 1348.

eyes were turned to the earth and their minds fixed on Heaven. Jealousy, malice, rancor, quarrels, suspicion, and bitterness had no place in them; instead, there was only great harmony, constant serenity, and actions of thanksgiving and praise.[154]

But he also reproached [the brothers] for the excessive harshness with which they treated their own bodies. In those times, the brothers gave themselves over to fasting, vigils, and hard physical work in order to totally repress the inducements toward carnality. They mistreated themselves so much that they seemed to hold themselves in hatred. In hearing and seeing such exaggerations, Francis rebuked them, as has been said, and commanded them to be moderate. He was so full of the grace and wisdom of the Savior that he admonished kindly, rebuked with good sense, and instructed with gentleness.[155]

In the early days of the Order, when Francis began to receive brothers, he lived with them near Rivotorto. One night, at midnight, while everyone was resting on their beds, a brother suddenly cried out, "I am dying! I am dying!" All the others awoke, amazed and terrified. Francis rose and said, "Get up, brothers, and light a

154 Celano, *First Life*, 393.

155 *Anonymous of Perugia*, 1532.

lamp." After the lamp was lit, the Saint asked, "Who yelled, 'I am dying?'" A friar replied, "It is I," to which Francis replied, "What is the matter, brother? What are you dying of?" And he replied, "I am dying of hunger."

Full of goodness and kindness, Francis immediately had the table prepared. So that the brother would not be ashamed to eat alone, they all sat down together and ate with him. Both that brother and the others had recently converted to the Lord, and they afflicted their bodies beyond measure.

After the meal, Francis spoke. He said, "Dear brothers, I recommend that each one of you take into account your own physical condition. If one of you can be sustained with less food than another, I do not want the one who needs more nourishment to try to imitate the other in this respect. Instead, each should be aware of his own constitution and provide what is necessary for his body. Just as we must refrain from excessive eating, which is harmful to body and soul, we should [refrain] from excessive abstinence all the more, since the Lord prefers mercy to sacrifice."[156]

---

156 *Legend of Perugia/Assisi Compilation*, 1545.

Creation

In every work, he praises the Craftsman; that is, he refers everything he sees in creatures to the Creator. He rejoices in all the works of the Lord's hands, and through this joyful vision, he intuits the cause and reason that vivifies them. In beautiful things, he recognizes the Supreme Beauty. From all that is good, a cry rises: "The One who created us is infinitely good." Through the footprints impressed in nature, he follows the Beloved everywhere and makes himself a ladder of everything to reach his throne. When the brothers cut wood, he forbids them to cut down the tree completely, so that it can shoot new shoots. He orders the gardener to leave the borders around the garden uncultivated so that, in due time, the green of the herbs and the splendor of the flowers will sing of the beauty of the Father of all creation. He also wants a flowerbed in the garden to be reserved for fragrant herbs that produce flowers so that those who observe them recall the memory of eternal sweetness. He even picks up small worms from the road so that they are not trampled. And he wants the bees to be fed honey and excellent wine so that they do not die of starvation in the harsh winter.[157]

Moreover, in consideration of the initial origin of all things, he referred to all creatures, however modest, with the name of Brother and Sister, considering that, together with him, they came from the same Origin. However, he embraced with greater passion and sweetness those [creatures] that by natural resemblance image the pious meekness of Christ and image [that meekness] through the meaning attributed to them by Scripture [that is, for example, lambs].[158]

The man of God was traveling through the Spoleto Valley for the purpose of preaching. When he came to a place near Bevagna, there was a very large quantity of birds of various kinds gathered. [Tradition has located the exact site as Pian d'Arca.] While he was observing them with a pious eye, he was filled with the Spirit of the Lord. He ran quickly to that place, greeted them with liveliness, and imposed silence on them so that they could listen attentively to the word of God.

While he was speaking to the birds and bringing forward many arguments to demonstrate the benefits that God has wrought for creatures and the praises

---

157 Celano, *Second Life*, 750.

158 Bonaventure, *Minor Legend*, 1353.

they should sing to Him, the birds, wriggling in a wonderful way, began to stretch their necks, spread their wings, open their beaks, and stare at him attentively as if they were trying to hear his admirable and effective discourses.

It was truly fitting that the God-filled man should feel drawn with a feeling of piety and humanity towards such irrational creatures, while they, in turn, felt drawn to him in such a wondrous way and were attentive when he instructed them and obeyed when he commanded.[159]

Since he was a simple man, not by nature but by divine grace, he began to accuse himself of negligence for not having preached before then to the birds, since they listened so devoutly to the word of God. From that day, he began to invite all birds, animals, reptiles, and even inanimate creatures to praise and love the Creator, since every day, invoking the name of the Lord, he realized from personal experience how obedient they were to him.[160]

---

159 Bonaventure, *Minor Legend*, 1371.

160 Celano, *First Life*, 425.

Fraternity

Like living stones, so to speak, gathered from every part of the world, [the friars] grew into a temple of the Holy Spirit. How ardent was the fraternal love of the new disciples of Christ! How strong was their love for their religious family! Every time that in some place, for example, on the street, as it happened, they passed one another, there was a true explosion of spiritual affection, the only love that above all other loves is the source of true fraternal charity. There were chaste embraces, delicate feelings, holy kisses, sweet conversations, modest smiles, a happy appearance, a simple eye, a humble soul, courteous speech, kind answers, full unanimity in their ideal, ready homage, and tireless mutual service. Having despised all earthly things and being free from any selfish love, since [the friars] poured out all the affection of their hearts on the bosom of the community, they tried with all their might to give even of themselves to meet the needs of other brothers. They were happy when they encountered one another and happier when they were staying together. It was hard for all to live apart and bitter and painful to part. These most docile soldiers, however, preferred nothing to the commands of holy obedience; rather, they prepared themselves for it in advance and rushed to carry out whatever was ordered of them, without question and with every obstacle removed.[161]

They were very virtuous men, devoted to God, dear to the saints in Heaven and beloved by men on earth. Upon them, blessed Francis rested like a house on four pillars. I omit their names out of respect for their modesty, a virtue which, as true religious, they cherish most cordially. Modesty is in fact the decorum of all ages, a witness of innocence, a sign of a pure heart, a rod of discipline, a special glory of the conscience, a guarantee of good reputation, and the value and crown of perfect rectitude. This virtue was common to them and rendered them pleasing and lovable to all. Each had his own virtue: the first was particularly discreet, the second was wonderfully patient, the third of commendable simplicity, and the last was robust in body and gentle in spirit. With all diligence, care, and good will, they defended the spiritual recollection of the blessed father and cared for his illness without sparing themselves pains and toils, happy to dedicate themselves totally to his service.[162]

---

161 Celano, *First Life*, 387.

162 Celano, *First Life*, 499.

Deeply humble and mature in charity, each one had for his brother the sentiments one has toward a father or lord. Those who had a preeminent role in the fraternity due to the offices they held or personal qualities made themselves the humblest and smallest of all. Each was disposed to the most generous obedience, always available to the will of the superior, without asking whether the order received was just or not because all were convinced that any command was in accordance with the dispositions of the Lord. In this way, it was easy and sweet to carry out any and all precepts.[163]

Prayer

At that time, the brothers earnestly asked [Francis] to teach them how to pray because they were simple in spirit and did not yet know the liturgical office. He answered, "When you pray, say the Our Father and, 'We adore you, Lord Jesus Christ, here and in all your churches in the whole world, and we bless you, because by your holy cross you have redeemed the world.'" The disciples of the pious master strove to observe this with all diligence, for they intended to carry out perfectly

163 *Legend of the Three Companions*, 1488.

not only his fraternal counsels and commands but even his secret thoughts, if they could in any way divine them.[164]

They almost never ceased to pray and praise the Lord. Examining all their actions, they thanked God for the good they had done and wept bitterly for the sins and negligence they had committed.[165]

The servant of Christ, living in the body, felt himself in exile from the Lord, while on the outside, for love of Christ, he had become totally insensitive to the desires of the world. By praying without ceasing, he strove to keep his spirit in the presence of God so as not to remain deprived of the consolation of the Beloved. Walking and sitting, indoors and out, working and resting, he remained so intent on prayer that it seemed as if he had devoted every part of himself to it: not only his heart and body but also his activity and time. Many times he was overwhelmed by such an excess of devotion that, raptured above himself and going beyond the limits of human sensitivity, he was totally unaware of what was happening outside or around him.[166]

---

164 Celano, *First Life*, 399.

165 Celano, *First Life*, 391.

166 Bonaventure, *Minor Legend*, 1357.

He always sought a secluded place where he could unite himself, not only with his spirit but with his entire body, with his God. If he suddenly felt visited by the Lord, so as not to be left without a cell, he made a small one with his cloak. If at times he was without his cloak, he covered his face with his sleeve so as not to reveal the hidden manna.[167]

He said, "There are many brothers who day and night put all their passion and care into acquiring knowledge while neglecting their holy vocation and devout prayer. When they announce the Gospel to an individual person or to a crowd, if they see or hear that some have been edified or converted to penance, they become puffed up and inflated with pride because of the results obtained by the labor of others. Indeed, those whom they imagine they have edified or converted to penance with their speeches, it is the Lord who edifies and converts thanks to the prayers of the holy brothers, even if the latter are unaware of it. This is the will of God: that they do not realize it, so as not to become proud."[168]

In this way, he directed all his mind and affection to that one thing he asked of God: he was not so much

---

167 Celano, *Second Life*, 681.

168 *Legend of Perugia/Assisi Compilation*, 1624.

a man who prayed, as he himself was completely transformed into living prayer.[169]

Charity

It was his earnest desire that both he and the brothers should abound in good works, through which the Lord is praised. He said, "Have the peace that you proclaim with your mouth even more abundantly in your hearts. Do not provoke anyone to anger or scandal, but let everyone be drawn to peace, goodness, and harmony by your meekness. This is our vocation: to heal wounds, bind up fractures, and call back the lost. Many who seem to us to be members of the devil can one day become disciples of Christ."[170]

During the day, the able-bodied engaged in manual labor or [worked] in leper shelters or in other dignified places, serving all with humility and devotion. They did not want to perform any work that could give rise to scandal; rather, they always occupied themselves with holy, just, honest, and useful things, giving an example

169 Celano, *Second Life*, 682.

170 *Legend of the Three Companions*, 1469.

of humility and patience to all those with whom they found themselves.[171]

The Source of mercy had poured out a sweet compassion in the servant of the Lord with such abundance and fullness that in relieving the miseries of the wretched, he seemed to bear within himself the heart of a mother. Clemency was also innate to him, which the piety of Christ, infused from above, redoubled. Thus, he felt his soul melt for the sick and the poor, and he offered them his affection when he could not offer his hand. This was because he offered whatever form of impoverishment or deprivation he saw in someone, with the sweetness of his pious heart, to Christ. In all the poor, he saw the face of Christ. Therefore, if something necessary for sustenance was given to him, whenever he met the poor, he not only generously offered it to them, he also judged that it should be returned to them, as if it actually belonged to them. He withheld absolutely nothing: cloaks, tunics, books, and even altar furnishings. Whenever he could, he gave everything to the needy. He even sought to completely consume himself in order to fully realize the duty of perfect piety.[172]

---

171 Celano, *First Life*, 389.

172 Bonaventure, *Minor Legend*, 1354.

While he was staying at Our Lady of the Portiuncula, a poor, elderly woman, who had two sons in the Order, came to ask blessed Francis for alms. The Saint immediately said to Brother Peter of Catanii, "Can we find something to offer our mother?" He used to say that the mother of a brother was his mother and the mother of all the brothers. Peter answered him, "There is nothing at home that we can give her, because she would like an alms with which to feed herself. In the church, we have only a New Testament, from which we read during matins." At that time, the brothers did not have breviaries or many psalters. Francis concluded, "Then give our mother the New Testament so that she can sell it to meet her needs. I firmly believe that this gesture will please God and the Blessed Virgin more than reading to us." And so he gave it to her.[173]

These are the principles with which Francis educated his new sons—not simply with words but above all with the works and example of his life.[174]

---

173 *Mirror of Perfection*, 1724.

174 Celano, *First Life*, 393.

Evangelization *Ad Mundum*

May 14, AD 1217

At the first general chapter held at the Portiuncula, twelve provinces were established, including beyond the Alps and in the Holy Land.

Eleven years after the founding of the Order, the friars having grown in number and merit, ministers were chosen and sent together with groups of friars to virtually every part of the world where the Catholic faith is present.[175]

Late May, AD 1217

When Francis arrived in Florence, he found Hugolino, bishop of Ostia [and future protector of the Order], who later became Pope [Gregory IX]. [. . .]

175 *Legend of the Three Companions*, 1475.

When he heard from Francis that he intended to go to France, he forbade him from making the journey, saying to him, "Brother, I do not want you to go beyond the Alps because in the Roman Curia there are numerous prelates and other people who would willingly harm the good of your Order. I and other cardinals who esteem your movement protect it wholeheartedly and shall help it, provided that you do not leave this region."

Francis responded, "Lord, it is sad for me to remain in these provinces after I have sent my brothers to distant and foreign lands."

The bishop replied with a reproachful tone, "So why did you send your brothers so far away? So they would die of hunger and other tribulations?"

The Saint answered with great enthusiasm of spirit and prophecy, "Do not think, Lord, that the Lord has sent the brothers only for the good of these regions. I tell you in truth that God has chosen and sent the brothers for the spiritual benefit and salvation of the souls of men throughout the world. They will be received not only in the lands of the Christians but also in those of the infidels. As long as they observe what they have promised the Lord, God will give them what they need in the lands of the infidels as well as in the Christian ones."

Hugolino was greatly amazed by Francis's words, and he declared that he was telling the truth. All the same, he did not allow him to go to France. The Saint then sent Brother Pacifico there with other brothers and returned to the Spoleto Valley.[176]

In some regions, [the friars] were welcomed but were not allowed to build [permanent] homes. In other places, they were driven out because they were feared to be heretics. In fact, the Pope had not confirmed their Rule but only granted it provisionally. Therefore, they suffered many tribulations on behalf of ecclesiastics and laymen alike and were despoiled by robbers. Many returned to Saint Francis bitter and dejected. They suffered similar hardships in Hungary, Germany, and other regions beyond the Alps.[177]

About sixty or perhaps more friars, led by John from Penna, were sent to Germany. After they had penetrated into the regions of Germany, they were asked if they wanted lodging, food, or other things of the kind. Not knowing the language, they replied, *Ja* [that is, "yes,"] and so they were kindly received by some. The friars

---

176 *Legend of Perugia/Assisi Compilation*, 1638.

177 *Anonymous of Perugia*, 1538.

soon noticed that they were treated humanely when using this word *Ja*. Therefore, they decided to answer *Ja* to anything that was asked of them. Some time later, they were questioned as to whether they were heretics and whether they had come specifically to contaminate Germany just as they had perverted Lombardy. Again, they answered *Ja*. Some were promptly imprisoned, while others were stripped and led around naked and made a comic spectacle for the crowd. Upon seeing that the friars did not produce fruits in Germany, they returned to Italy. For this reason, Germany was considered so inhumane by the friars that they did not dare return unless animated by the desire for martyrdom.[178]

The friars who arrived in France were asked if they were Albigensians. [Editor: The Albigensians were a heretical group also known as Cathars.] They replied yes, not understanding what Albigensians were, that is, that they were heretics. And so [the friars] were considered heretics. But the bishops and the teachers, in the end, after having carefully read their Rule and finding it evangelical and Catholic, consulted Pope Honorius on the matter. As a result, because of [the pope's] letters, their Rule was declared authentic. In fact, it had

178 Jordan of Giano, *Chronicle*, 2327.

been approved by the Apostolic See, and the friars were [considered] special sons of the Roman Church and true Catholics. In this way, they were freed from the suspicion of heresy.[179]

June 11, AD 1218

In a papal bull, Pope Honorius assures the bishops of the catholicity of the Friars Minor.

"Since the beloved sons, Brother Francis and his companions, who belong to the life and religion of the Friars Minor, after having abandoned the vanities of this world, have chosen a way of life deservedly approved by the Roman Church, and they exhaust themselves going throughout the diverse parts of the world in the example of the Apostles sowing the seed of the word of God, We therefore beseech and exhort all of you in the Lord, and by these apostolic letters command you, when members of the aforesaid brotherhood present themselves to you bearing these letters, to receive them as [true] Catholic faithful, showing yourselves favorable and kind to them out of reverence for God and for Us."[180]

---

179 Jordan of Giano, *Chronicle*, 2326.

180 Honorius III, Bull *Cum dilecti*, 2708.

Finally, we have contemplated this vineyard, which having grown in a very short time, spread its fruitful branches from sea to sea. From every side, multitudes of men have come in droves, and suddenly, the living stones have gathered for the perfect structure of this wonderful temple. And we see it not only multiplied in a short time in the number of children but also glorified. In fact, many of those whom it has generated, we know, have obtained the palm branch of martyrdom. And we venerate many of them in the register of the saints because of the perfect practice of virtue.[181]

Everyone can see the fervor of perfect charity by which the friend of the Bridegroom felt himself transported to God, above all from this: Saint Francis ardently desired to sacrifice himself with the flame of martyrdom, *a living host*, to God.[182]

---

181 Celano, *Treatise of Miracles*, 824.

182 Bonaventure, *Minor Legend*, 1356.

AD 1212

Francis makes two unsuccessful attempts to reach "Syria" to preach to the Muslims.

In the sixth year of his conversion [probably in 1212], burning with the desire for sacred martyrdom, he decided to go to Syria to preach faith and penance to the Saracens [that is, Muslims] and other infidels. He boarded a ship for that region, but because of contrary winds, he found himself with the other sailors in the regions of Slavonia. Disappointed in his ardent desire, a short time later, since there was no other ship leaving for Syria that year, he begged some sailors heading for Ancona to take him with them [and he returned to Italy]. [. . .] Having abandoned the sea, the servant of the Most High, Francis, now began to travel the earth, and furrowing it with the ploughshare of the word of God, he sowed there the seed of life, which produces blessed fruits. [. . .] But although, like the evangelical tree, he produced abundant and exquisite fruits, this was not enough to extinguish in Francis the sublime purpose and his ardent desire for martyrdom. And so, shortly afterward, he undertook a missionary journey to Morocco to announce the Good News to Miramolino [Editor: This is an Italianized version of the sultan's name, Emir-el-Mumenin] and his coreligionists. His apostolic desire was so strong that at times he left his traveling companion behind, hastening in the intoxication of his spirit to carry out his purpose. But the good God, who was pleased by his mere benignity to remember me and countless others, confronted Francis directly when he arrived in Spain so as not to let him continue further: an illness came upon him and forced him to interrupt the journey he had undertaken. [And he returned again to Italy.][183]

January 16, AD 1220

Five friars, known as the Franciscan Protomartyrs, are killed in Morocco after attempting to evangelize Muslims.

Of the friars, then, who passed through Spain, five were crowned with martyrdom. Whether these friars were sent after that chapter, which we have mentioned, or a previous one, in which Friar Elias and his companions [were sent] to the Lands beyond the Sea, we cannot say with assuredness.[184]

183 Celano, *First Life*, 418–420.

184 Jordan of Giano, *Chronicle*, 2329.

The protomartyrs were canonized by Pope Sixtus IV in 1481. Their saga is narrated in the 14th-century Passio Sancti Berardi.

[Francis is speaking to the friars:] "My children, the Lord has commanded me to send you to the lands of the Saracens to preach, to confess his Faith, and to fight the law of Mohammed. I, too, will go to the infidels, and I will send other brothers throughout the world. Come, my children, and prepare yourselves to do the will of the Lord." And they humbly bowed before him and answered, "Father, we are ready to obey you in everything." [. . .]

[The friars, speaking to the Muslim king:] "For this reason we speak these things mainly to you, in order to lead you and yours on the path of truth, in which you may finally be saved." At these words, the king was filled with anger, and he ordered their heads to be cut off.

The brothers, with joy on their faces, said to one another as they were being removed from his presence, "Come, brothers! We have found what we were looking for. Let us be steadfast and not fear to die for Christ!" [. . .]

At the news [that the five were martyred], Saint Francis exclaimed, "I can finally say that I have five true Minor Friars."[185]

Francis desires to evangelize the Muslim people.

Francis's excess of devotion and charity raised him to divine realities in such a way that his affectionate goodness expanded towards those whom nature and grace made his companions. There is no need to be surprised that just as the piety of his heart had made him a brother to all other creatures, so the charity of Christ made him even more intensely a brother to those who bear in themselves the image of the Creator and have been redeemed by the blood of the Redeemer.

Yet he did not consider himself a friend of Christ if he did not care lovingly for those souls redeemed by Him. Nothing, he said, should be placed before the salvation of souls, and he confirmed this statement above all with this argument: the Only Begotten of God, for souls, deigned to ascend the cross.[186]

---

185 *Passion of the Holy Martyrs, Brothers Berard, Peter, Adiuti, Accursio, and Otto in Morocco.*

186 Bonaventure, *Major Legend*, 1168.

Fall AD 1219

On the third attempt, Francis is successful at arriving in the Holy Land, where he meets the sultan.

[Francis] could not rest until he could more fervently fulfill the burning desire of his soul. So, in the thirteenth year of his conversion, he set out for Syria, where bitter and harsh battles were being fought every day between Christians [Crusaders] and pagans. Francis took a companion with him [Editor: St. Bonaventure names him as Brother Illuminato] and did not hesitate to present himself before the sultan of the Saracens [Malik al-Kamil]. Who could describe the courage with which Francis stood before him, the firmness with which he spoke, or the eloquence and decision with which he answered those who insulted the Christian law? Before reaching the sultan, his assassins seized Francis, insulted him, and whipped him. But he was not frightened by threats, torture, or death. Although invested with the hostile spirit and feelings of hatred of many, behold, he was welcomed by the sultan with great honor! [The sultan] lavished upon Francis royal favors and countless gifts in an effort to convert him to the riches of the world. However, seeing how Francis resolutely despises all material things as if rubbish, [the sultan] was deeply amazed, and he looked at him as different from all other men. Moreover, he was quite moved by his words, and he listened to him quite willingly. But despite all these circumstances, the Lord did not fulfill Francis's desire [for martyrdom], and he reserved for him the privilege of a singular grace. [Editor: Celano is referring to the future reception of the stigmata.][187]

---

187 Celano, *First Life*, 422.

From Travails to Regulation

In 1209, what is known as the Protorule was orally approved by Pope Innocent III. From that point on, Francis and the friars met annually to modify and improve their form of life, expressed in the Rule. While St. Francis was in the Holy Land from 1219 to 1220, various crises developed in the Order, including attempts on behalf of the erudite friars to mitigate the harshness of the form of life envisioned by Francis. This led him to return to Italy. The pope promptly assigned Bishop Hugolino as the Order's protector, and Francis set out to formalize the Rule. The first attempt is what is known as the Rule of 1221, also known as the Earlier Rule or the Regula non bullata. *Finally, in 1223, Francis wrote the Rule of 1223, the Later Rule, or the* Regula Bullata, *which was approved by Pope Honorius.*

Blessed Francis composed three Rules: the one confirmed by Pope Innocent III [in 1209], but without the papal bull; a second, shorter one [of 1221], which was lost; and finally the [third] one, which Pope Honorius III approved with a bull [of 1223].[188]

A perfect zealot for the observance of the Holy Gospel, blessed Francis was ardently zealous that all [friars] put the Rule into practice, which is nothing other than the perfect observance of the Gospel, and he gave a special blessing to those who are and will be true zealots of it. He told his disciples that the Rule is the book of life, the hope of salvation, the pledge of glory, the marrow of the Gospel, the way of the cross, the state of perfection, the key to Heaven, and the pact of the eternal covenant. He wanted everyone to keep [a copy of] it and know it [by heart], and that the friars should speak of it frequently in their conversation to combat indolence, and that they should converse about it often interiorly to recall the promise they had made. He prescribed that they should keep the Rule always before their eyes as an admonition and reminder of their proposition of life and of the dutiful regular observance. Moreover, he wanted and taught that the friars should die with it.[189]

---

188 *Mirror of Perfection*, 1677.

189 *Mirror of Perfection*, 1771.

The Rule of 1209 is developed gradually by way of biannual chapters.

Blessed Francis established that a chapter should be celebrated twice a year there [at St. Mary of the Angels]: at Pentecost and on the feast of the dedication of Saint Michael in September [29]. At Pentecost, all the friars gathered at St. Mary's and discussed how they could better observe the Rule [of 1209]. [. . .] Saint Francis spoke to the friars about the admonitions, rebukes, and directives that seemed to him to be in accordance with the will of God. Everything he expressed to them in words, he demonstrated with care and affection in his comportment.[190]

AD 1219–1220

While St. Francis is in the Holy Land, the vicars in charge begin relaxing the Rule.

Now, since according to the Protorule [of 1209], the friars fasted [according to a strict discipline], these two vicars, with some of the older friars from all over Italy, celebrated a chapter in which they established [more lax norms regarding fasting]. A lay friar,

190 *Legend of the Three Companions*, 1466.

indignant at these constitutions because they had had the presumption of adding to the holy father's Rule, took those constitutions with him, without the authorization of the vicars, across the sea [to the Holy Land]. When he arrived in the presence of blessed Francis, the first thing he did was confess his guilt, asking forgiveness for having come without permission. However, he was induced by necessity—that is, because the vicars, whom he had left, had the presumption of adding new norms to his Rule. He also informed Francis that the Order throughout Italy was in turmoil, both because of the vicars and because of other friars who were demanding other innovations.[191]

AD 1219–1220

Francis returns to Italy.

At that time, there lived overseas a [seer] who foresaw many events that were true; for this reason, she was called "the Truthful One" in that language. She said to the brothers who were with Francis, "Return! Return [to Italy]! Because of the absence of Brother Francis, the Order is troubled, divided, and dispersed." And

191 Jordan of Giano, *Chronicle*, 2333–2334.

this was true. [. . .] In addition to these unfortunate events, during the absence of blessed Francis, other causes of disturbance had also arisen, just as the Truthful One had predicted. Therefore, blessed Francis took with him Brother Elias, Brother Peter of Catanii, and Brother Cesario [. . .] and returned to Italy. Once in Italy, after having thoroughly understood the causes of the disturbances, he went not to the agitators but to the Lord Pope Honorius.[192]

Francis wants the Order to remain under the Roman Church.

Francis said, "I will go and entrust the Order of the Minor Brothers to the Roman Church. The malevolent will be intimidated and held in check by the strength of her authority, and the children of God will enjoy perfect freedom to the increase of eternal salvation. From this, the children will recognize the sweet benefits of their mother and will always follow her venerable footsteps with particular devotion."[193]

---

192 Jordan of Giano, *Chronicle*, 2335–2337.

193 *Mirror of Perfection*, 1773.

Summer AD 1220

Cardinal Hugolino is appointed Protector of the Order.

[Francis] went to Rome, where the Lord Pope Honorius and all the cardinals received him with great devotion. [. . .] Having finished his speech and after a few moments of cordial conversation with the pope, he finally presented his request as follows: "It is not easy, Lord, as you know, for poor and humble people [like me] to have access to such great majesty. You have the world in your hands, and very important commitments do not allow you to dedicate yourself to minutiae. For this reason, Lord, I ask the most tender affection of your holiness to grant us as pope [that is, protector] the lord [bishop] of Ostia, who is present here. Thus, with the dignity of your preeminence remaining always intact, the friars will be able to turn to him in times of need and be advantageously defended and governed." [. . .] The Pope was pleased with such a holy request, and he immediately appointed Lord Hugolino, then bishop of Ostia, as head of the Order, according to the request of the man of God.[194]

---

194 Celano, *Second Life*, 612.

Francis then gave thanks to God and replied [to Bishop Hugolino], "Lord, I am happy to have you as father and protector of our Order, and I want you, for the love of God, to always remember me in your prayers." Then he asked him to attend the chapter that was to be celebrated at Pentecost. The cardinal acquiesced immediately and heartily. From that time on, he participated in the friars' chapter assembly every year.[195]

AD 1220

Due to his worsening health, difficulty in administration, and desire to spend more time in prayer, Francis steps down from leadership, appointing Peter of Catanii as Vicar.

To preserve the virtue of holy humility, a few years after his conversion, in the presence of all during a chapter, Francis renounced the office of governing the Order. He said, "From today forward, I have died to you. But behold Brother Peter of Catanii, whom I and all of you must obey." Then, bowing down immediately before him, Francis promised him "obedience and reverence." The friars openly wept and burst into loud

---

195 *Legend of the Three Companions*, 1474.

groans of grief, seeing themselves as if they had become orphans of such a father. [. . .] From that moment, Francis remained a subject until his death, behaving more humbly than any other friar.[196]

AD 1221

Francis writes a second Rule, which is believed to have been presented at the Chapter of Mats of 1221.

And so, with the favor of God, the turbulence was immediately calmed, and blessed Francis restructured the Order according to his ordinances. Upon seeing that Brother Ceasar [of Speyer] was an expert in Sacred Scripture, he entrusted to him the task of adorning the Rule with words of the Gospel, which he did in simple words.

Now, various rumors had spread about blessed Francis—some said that he was dead, others that he had been killed, still others that he had drowned. Thus, a great many of the brothers were amazed when they learned that he was alive and that he had already returned [from the Holy Land]. They felt joyfully as if a new light had dawned. Blessed Francis then,

196 Celano, *Second Life*, 727.

without delay, called a general chapter at St. Mary of the Portiuncula.[197]

May 30, AD 1221

During the general chapter of 1221, known as the Chapter of Mats, significant tensions surface regarding the Rule.

While Francis was at the general chapter, called the Chapter of Mats, which was held at the Portiuncula and in which five thousand brothers were present, many of them—men of culture—approached, approached Cardinal Hugolino, the future Gregory IX, who in turn was participating in the chapter assembly. They asked him to persuade Francis to follow the advice of the learned brothers and to sometimes let himself be guided by them. They referred to the Rules of St. Benedict, St. Augustine, and St. Bernard, which prescribe this and that norm for the purpose of leading a well-ordered religious life.

When Francis heard the cardinal's exhortation on this subject, he took him by the hand and led him before the chapter assembly and said, "My brothers,

---

197 Jordan of Giano, *Chronicle*, 2338.

God has called me to walk the path of simplicity that He has shown to me. I do not want you to assign to me any other Rule—neither that of Saint Augustine, nor that of Saint Bernard, nor that of Saint Benedict. The Lord has revealed to me that it is His will that I should be as a fool in the world. This is the knowledge to which God wants us to commit ourselves! He will confuse you by means of your own knowledge and wisdom. I have confidence in the Lord's stewards, whom He will use to punish you. Then, willingly or unwillingly, you will return with great shame to your vocation."

The cardinal was astonished at these words and said nothing. And all the friars were filled with holy fear.[198]

Blessed Francis was greatly troubled when one [of his friars], in neglect of virtue, went in search of knowledge that puffs up, especially if a friar did not persist in the vocation to which he had been called from the beginning. He said, "My friars who are seized by the curiosity of knowledge will find themselves empty handed on the day of tribulation. Therefore, I would like them to strengthen themselves in virtue. Then, when the time of tribulation comes, they will have the Lord with them in their anguish. And, in

198 *Legend of Perugia/Assisi Compilation*, 1673.

fact, the tribulation is also about to come, and those books, which will then be of no use, will be thrown out of the windows and into the closets." He did not say this because he disliked reading the Holy Scriptures but to distract them all from the superfluous concern of learning. He wanted the brothers to be worthy of charity rather than be know-it-alls through curiosity about knowledge. He also sensed and foresaw that the time was not far off when that knowledge that puffs up would be the cause of ruin.[199]

Francis is afflicted with a long temptation.

As Francis's merits grew, so did his disagreement with the ancient serpent. The greater his charisms, the more subtle the attempts and the more violent the attacks against him. And although [the devil] had often known him by experience as a valiant warrior who did not fail even for an instant in combat, nevertheless he still tried to attack him, even though the latter always emerged victorious.[200]

He was so afflicted by this [temptation] in mind and body that many times he withdrew from the

199 *Mirror of Perfection*, 1762.

200 Celano, *Second Life*, 702.

company of the brothers because he was not joyful as usual. He mortified himself, however, by abstaining from food, drink, and speech, and he prayed more insistently and shed more abundant tears so that the Lord would deign to send him an effective remedy in such grave tribulation. Having lived in such anguish for more than two years, one day, while he was praying in the church of St. Mary of the Angels, it happened that the words of the Gospel were spoken to him in spirit, "If you had faith as a grain of a mustard seed and ordered that a mountain be moved, it would be so" (see Mt 17:19, translated from the original text) Immediately blessed Francis answered, "Lord, which mountain is this?" And it was said to him, "That mountain is your temptation." Blessed Francis responded, "Then, Lord, let it be done to me as you have said!" Immediately he was delivered so perfectly that it seemed to him as if he had never suffered any temptation.[201]

AD 1223

St. Francis decides to write the third and final Rule.

---

201 *Mirror of Perfection*, 1798.

By now, the Order had spread greatly, and so Francis intended to have Pope Honorius confirm in perpetuity the form of life already approved [orally in 1209] by his predecessor, Pope Innocent. God encouraged Francis in this purpose through a revelation. In this way, he seemed to see that he had collected from the ground some very small crumbs of bread to distribute to many hungry friars who were around him. He was afraid that, in distributing them, those very small crumbs might perhaps fall from his hand. But a voice from above said to him, "Francis, take all these crumbs and make a single host to offer to whomever wishes to eat of it." While he was doing this, all those who did not receive the gift with devotion or, after receiving it, despised it, immediately distinguished themselves from the others by becoming lepers.

In the morning, the Saint told his companions about the vision, regretting that he did not understand its meaning. But the next day, while he was praying with great perseverance, he heard this voice come from Heaven, "Francis, the crumbs you saw last night are the words of the Gospel, the host is the Rule, and the leprosy is iniquity."[202]

---

202 Bonaventure, *Major Legend*, 1082.

Spring–summer AD 1223

At Fonte Colombo, near Rieti, Francis composes a final Rule for the friars, which is approved by Pope Honorius. For this reason, it is known as the Regula Bullata, *or the Rule of 1223.*

Following the indications he had received in vision, before having the Rule approved, he wanted to reduce it to a more compendious form, which he had drawn up with long and abundant quotations from the Gospel. Therefore, guided by the Holy Spirit, he went up a mountain [Fonte Colombo] with two companions. There, fasting on bread and water, he dictated the Rule, according to what the divine Spirit suggested to him during prayer. [. . .] He then obtained that it be confirmed, as he had desired, by the aforementioned Pope Honorius in the eighth year of his pontificate [on November 29, AD 1223]. To encourage the friars to observe it fervently, he said that he had not put anything of his own into it but had written everything down as revealed to him by God.[203]

While in Fonte Colombo, the ministers came to Francis with a request to relax the Rule.

---

203 Bonaventure, *Major Legend*, 1083–1084.

Francis lived on a mountain together with Brother Leo of Assisi and Boniface of Bologna to compose the Rule, since the text of the first, dictated to him by Christ, had been lost. Many ministers went to Brother Elias, the vicar of Francis, and said to him, "We have heard that Brother Francis is making a new Rule, and we fear that he will make it so harsh that it will be unobservable. We want you to go to him and tell him that we refuse to submit to this Rule. Let him write it for himself and not for us." Brother Elias replied that he did not have the courage to go to Francis for fear of his rebuke. But when they insisted, he replied that he would not go there without them. So they all set out together. When Brother Elias, accompanied by the ministers, arrived at Fonte Colombo, he called the Saint. Francis went out and, seeing the ministers, asked, "What do these brothers want?"

Elias answered, "They are ministers. They learned that you are making a new Rule and fear that it is too harsh. They protest that they do not intend to be bound by it. Write it for yourself and not for them."

Francis raised his face to Heaven and spoke to Christ, "Lord, did I not say that they would not believe you?"

Immediately, the voice of Christ could be heard in the air: "Francis, nothing of yours is in the Rule; rather, every prescription contained within it is mine. I want it to be observed to the letter, to the letter, to the letter! Without comments, without comments, without comments! I know well how much human weakness can do but also how much my grace can do. Therefore, those who do not want to observe the Rule should leave the Order!"

Francis then turned to those friars and said, "Did you hear? Did you hear? Do you want me to make you repeat it?" Thus, the ministers went away, scorned and acknowledging their guilt.[204]

November 29, AD 1223

Pope Honorius approves the Rule,
known as the Regula Bullata, *or the Rule of 1223.*

"The Apostolic See usually acquiesces benevolently to the pious and honest wishes of applicants. Therefore, beloved children in the Lord, we, inclined to your pious prayers, confirm to you with apostolic authority the Rule of your Order, approved by our predecessor

---

204 *Legend of Perugia/Assisi Compilation*, 167.

Innocent III, of good memory, transcribed in these letters, and we support it with the patronage of this writing. [. . .] Therefore, no one may violate this in any way."[205]

205 Honorius III, Bull *Solet annuere*, 2716.

Regula Bullata (The Rule of 1223)

November 29, AD 1223

Prologue

The Rule and life of the Friars Minor is this, namely, to observe the Holy Gospel of Our Lord Jesus Christ by living in obedience, without anything of one's own, and in chastity.

Brother Francis promises obedience and reverence to the Lord Pope Honorius and his canonically elected successors and to the Roman Church; and the other friars are bound to obey Brother Francis and his successors.

Concerning those who wish to adopt this life, and how they should be received

If any would desire to adopt this life and would come to our brothers, let them send them to their ministers provincial, to whom alone, and not to others, is the permission to receive friars conceded. Let the ministers indeed examine them diligently concerning the Catholic Faith and the sacraments of the Church.

And if they believe these things and want to observe them faithfully and firmly unto the end, and they have no wives or, if they do, their wives have already entered a monastery, or having taken a vow of continence, permission [to enter one] has been granted to them by authority of the bishop of the diocese, and the wives are of such an age that suspicion cannot arise concerning them, let them say unto these the word of the Holy Gospel (see Mt 19:21), that they should go and sell all that is their own and strive to give it to the poor. But if they cannot do this, a good will suffices for them.

And let the friars and their ministers beware lest they be solicitous concerning their temporal things, so that they may freely do with their own things whatever the Lord will have inspired them. If, however, counsel is required, let the ministers have permission to send them to other God-fearing men, by whose counsel their goods may be spent [*erogentur*] on the poor. Afterwards, let them grant them the clothes of probation, that is, two tunics without a capuche, a cord, breeches, and a chaperone[extending] to the cord, unless it seems to the same ministers [that it should be] otherwise according to God. Having truly finished the year of probation, let them be received to obedience, promising to always observe this life and Rule.

And in no manner will it be licit for them to go forth from this religious institute [*de ista religione exire*], according to the command of the Lord Pope, because according to the Holy Gospel "No one putting hand to the plow and turning back is fit for the Kingdom of God" (Lk 9:62, translated from the original text).

And let those who have already promised obedience have a tunic with a capuche, and if they wish to have it, another without a capuche. And let those who are driven by necessity be able to wear footwear. And let all the friars wear cheap clothing and be able to patch these with sackcloth and other pieces with the blessing of God. I warn and exhort them not to despise nor judge men whom they see clothed with soft and colored clothes, using dainty food and drink, but rather let each one judge and despise his very self.

Concerning the divine office and fasting; and in what manner the brothers ought to go through the world

Clerics are to perform [*faciant*] the divine office according to the Ordo of the Holy Roman Church, except for the psalter, for which they can have breviaries.

Let the laymen indeed say twenty-four *Our Fathers* for Matins; for Lauds five; for Prime, Terce, Sext and None, for each of these seven, for Vespers, however, twelve; for Compline seven; and let them pray for the dead.

And let them fast from the Feast of All Saints until Christmas. Indeed, may those who voluntarily fast the holy lent that begins at Epiphany and for the forty days that follow, which the Lord consecrated with His own holy fast, be blessed by the Lord, and let those who do not wish [to do so] not be constrained. But let them fast the other [Lent] until the [day of the] Resurrection of the Lord.

At other times however, they are not bound to fast, except on Fridays. Indeed, in time of manifest necessity, the friars are not bound to the corporal fast.

Indeed, I counsel, warn, and exhort my friars in the Lord Jesus Christ, that when they go about through the world, they are not to quarrel nor contend in words (see 2 Tm 2:14), nor are they to judge others, but they are to be meek, peaceable and modest, meek and humble, speaking uprightly to all, as is fitting. And they should not ride horseback, unless they are driven [to do so] by manifest necessity or infirmity.

Into whatever house they may enter, first let them say, "Peace to this house" (Lk 10:5). And according to the Holy Gospel it is lawful to eat of any of the foods that are placed before them (see Lk 10:8).

That the brothers should not receive money

I firmly command all the friars, that in no manner are they to receive coins or money through themselves or through an interposed person. However, for the necessities of the infirm and for the clothing of the other friars, only the ministers and the custodes are to conduct a solicitous care, by means of spiritual friends, according to places and seasons and cold regions, as they see expedites necessity; with this always preserved, that, as has been said, they do not receive coins nor money.

On the manner of working

Let those friars, to whom the Lord gives the grace to work, work faithfully and devotedly, in such a way that, having excluded idleness, the enemy of the soul, they do not extinguish the spirit of holy prayer and devotion, which all other temporal things should zealously serve [*deservire*]. Indeed, concerning the wages of labor, let them receive for themselves and for their friars what is for the necessity of the body, except coins or money, and this [they should do] humbly, as befits the servants of God and the followers of most holy poverty.

That the friars are to appropriate nothing for themselves, and concerning the begging of alms and sick friars

Let the friars appropriate nothing for themselves, neither house nor place, nor any thing. And as pilgrims and exiles (see 1 Pt 2:11) in this age, let them go about for alms confidently, as ones serving the Lord in poverty and humility, nor is it proper that they be ashamed [to do so], since the Lord made Himself poor in this world for us (see 2 Cor 8:9). This is that loftiness of most high poverty that has established you, my most dear friars, as heirs and kings of the Kingdom of Heaven, making you poor in things, it has raised you high in virtues (see Jas 2:5). Let this be your portion that leads you into the land of the living (see Ps 141(142):6). Cleaving totally to this, most beloved friars, may you want to have nothing other under heaven in perpetuity, for the [sake of] the Name of Our Lord Jesus Christ.

And, wherever the friars are and find themselves, let them mutually show themselves to be among their family members. And let them without fear manifest to one another their own need since, if a mother nourishes and loves her own son (see 1 Thes 2:7) according to the flesh, how much more diligently should he love and nourish his own spiritual brother?

And, if any of them should fall into infirmity, the other friars should care for him as they would want to be cared for themselves.

On the penance to be imposed on friars who are sinning

If any of the friars, at the instigation of the enemy, should sin mortally, for those sins, concerning which it has been ordained among the friars that one have recourse to the ministers provincial alone, the aforesaid friars are bound to have recourse to them as soon as they can, without delay. Indeed, let the ministers themselves, if they are priests, with mercy enjoin upon them a penance; if indeed they are not priests, let them have it enjoined by other priests of the Order, as it will seem to them to better expedite [the matter] according to

God. And they should beware not to grow angry and be distressed on account of the sin of another, since anger and distress impede charity in themselves and in others.

On the election of the minister general of this fraternity; and on the Chapter at Pentecost

All the friars are bound to always have one of the friars of this very same religion as minister general and servant of the whole fraternity, and they are bound firmly to obey him. When he dies, let an election of a successor be made by the ministers provincial and the custodes in the Pentecost Chapter, in which the ministers provincial are bound to convene at once [or at the same time], wherever it will have been determined by the minister general; and this once every three years or at another interval greater or less as it will have been ordained by the aforesaid minister.

And if at any time it may appear to all the ministers provincial and to the custodes that the aforesaid minister is not sufficient for the service and common utility of the friars, the aforesaid friars, to whom the electing has been given, are bound in the Name of the Lord to choose another as their guardian [*in custodem*]. Indeed, after the Pentecost Chapter, let the ministers and custodes each be able, if they want and if it will seem to be expedient for them, once in the same year to call their friars together in chapter in their own custodies.

On preachers

Let the friars not preach in the diocese of any bishop when he has spoken against their [preaching]. And let no friar at all [*penitus*] dare preach to the people unless he will have been examined by the minister general of this fraternity and approved, and there be conceded to him by the same the office of preaching.

I also warn and exhort these same friars that in the preaching that they do, their expressions be considered and chaste (see Ps 11(12):7; 17(18):21), for [sake of] the utility and edification of the people, by announcing to them vices and virtues, punishment and glory with brevity of speech; since a brief word did the Lord speak upon the earth (see Rom 9:28).

On the admonition and correction of the friars

Let the friars who are ministers and servants of the other friars visit and warn their friars and humbly and charitably correct them, not commanding them anything that is contrary to their soul and our Rule. Indeed, let the friars who are subjects remember that for the sake of God they have renounced their own wills. Whence I firmly command them to obey their ministers in all things that they have promised the Lord to observe and that are not contrary to their soul or to our Rule. And wherever the friars are who know and understand that they themselves are not able to observe the Rule spiritually, they should and can have recourse to their ministers. Indeed, let the ministers receive them charitably and kindly and be so familiar with them that they can speak to them and act as lords with their servants; for so it should be, because the ministers are the servants of all the friars.

Indeed, I warn and exhort the friars in the Lord Jesus Christ, that they beware of all pride, vain glory, envy, avarice (see Lk 12:15), care and solicitude for this age, detraction and murmuring, and that those who are ignorant of letters not care to learn letters; but let them strive so that above all things they should desire to have the Spirit of the Lord and His holy operation, to pray always to Him with a pure heart and to have humility, [and] patience in persecution and in infirmity, and to love those who persecute and correct and accuse us, because the Lord says, "Love your enemies, pray for those who persecute and calumniate you" (Mt 5:44); "Blessed are those who suffer persecution for justice's sake, for theirs is the kingdom of heaven" (Mt 5:10); "He who has persevered until the end, however, will be saved" (Mt 10:22, translated from the original text).

That the brothers should not enter the monasteries of nuns

I firmly command all the brothers not to have suspicious company or conversation with women and not to enter the monasteries of nuns, except those [friars] to whom special permission has been conceded by the Apostolic See; neither are they to be godfathers of men or women [so that] scandal may not arise on this account among the friars nor concerning them.

Concerning those going among the Saracens and other infidels

Let whoever of the friars who by divine inspiration wants to go among the Saracens and other infidels seek permission for that reason from their minister provincial. Indeed, the ministers are to grant permission to go to no one except those who seem to be fit to be sent.

For which sake I enjoin the ministers by obedience to seek from the Lord Pope one of the cardinals of the Roman Church who is to be the governor, protector, and corrector of this fraternity, so that always subject and prostrate at the feet of this same Holy Church, stable in the Catholic Faith (see Col 1:23), we may observe what we have firmly promised: the poverty and humility and the Holy Gospel of Our Lord Jesus Christ.

The Confirmation of the Rule

Let it not be in any way licit to anyone among men to infringe this page of our confirmation, or to contravene it with rash daring. If anyone, however, would presume to attempt this, let him know himself to have incurred the indignation of the Omnipotent God and of Blessed Peter and Paul, His Apostles.

Given at the Lateran, on the third day of the Kalends of December, in the eight year of Our Pontificate.[206]

---

206 St. Francis, *The Rule of 1223*.

Part IV: Holiness

Conformity to Christ

First, it is to be considered that the glorious Messer Saint Francis was conformed to the blessed Christ in all acts of his life.[207]

December 24–25, AD 1223

Francis reenacts the Christmas Mass at Greccio, initiating the tradition of the creche.

In this regard, what the Saint accomplished three years before his glorious death, in Greccio, on the day of the Lord's nativity, is worthy of everlasting memory and devout celebration. In that region, there was a man named John. He was of good reputation and even better life, and he was very dear to blessed Francis because, although he was noble and highly honored in his region, he esteemed the nobility of the spirit more

207 *The Little Flowers*, 1826.

than that of the flesh. About two weeks before the feast of the Nativity, blessed Francis, as he often did, called upon him and said, “If you want us to celebrate the birth of Jesus in Greccio, go before me and prepare what I tell you: I would like to represent the Child born in Bethlehem and, in some way, see with the eyes of the body the hardships in which he found himself for lack of necessary things for a newborn, how he was laid in a manger, and how he lay on the hay between the ox and the donkey.” As soon as he heard him, the faithful and pious friend went quickly to prepare everything necessary in the designated place, according to the plan espoused by the Saint.

Finally, the day of joy arrives—the time of exultation! For the occasion, many friars are summoned here from various regions. Local men and women from farmhouses joyfully prepare candles and torches—each in accordance with his means—to illuminate that night, in which the Star that illuminated all days and times was lit splendidly in the sky.

Then, Francis arrives and sees that everything is arranged according to his desire, and he is radiant with joy. Then the manger is arranged, hay is placed in it, and the ox and the donkey are brought in. In that moving scene, evangelical simplicity shines, poverty is praised, and humility is recommended. Greccio has become like a new Bethlehem.

This night is as clear as broad daylight and sweet to men and animals! People flock and rejoice before the new mystery with a joy they have never tasted before. The forest resounds with voices, and the imposing rocks echo the festive choirs. The friars sing select praises to the Lord, and the night seems completely a leap of joy.

The Saint is there, ecstatic before the crib, his spirit vibrant with compunction and ineffable joy. Then the priest solemnly celebrates the Eucharist over the crib, and he himself savors a consolation never tasted before. Francis wears the vestments of a Levite because he was a deacon, and he sings the holy Gospel with a sonorous voice: that strong and sweet, clear and sonorous voice enraptures everyone with desire for Heaven. Then he speaks to the people. With the sweetest words, he recalls the newborn poor King and the little city of Bethlehem. Often, when he wanted to name Christ Jesus, inflamed with heavenly love, he called him "the Child of Bethlehem," and he pronounced that name "Bethlehem," filling his mouth with voice and even more with tender affection, producing a sound like the bleating of a sheep. And every time he said "Child of Bethlehem" or "Jesus," he passed his tongue over his lips, as if to taste and retain all the sweetness of those words.

The gifts of the Almighty were manifested in abundance. One of those present was a virtuous man who had a wondrous vision. It seemed to him that the Child was lying lifeless in the manger, and [he saw] Francis approach him and awake him from that sort of deep slumber. The prodigious vision was not in discordance with the facts. In fact, through the merits of the Saint, the Child Jesus was resurrected in the hearts of many who had forgotten him, and the memory of him remained deeply impressed in their memory. After that solemn vigil, each person returned home filled with ineffable joy.[208]

Francis and the brothers bear resemblance to the cross.

Since Saint Francis and his companions were called and chosen by God to bear with their hearts and actions and to preach with their tongues the cross of Christ, they seemed, and were, like crucified men as regards their habit, their austere life, and their acts and actions. Therefore, they desired more to endure shame and opprobrium for the love of Christ than worldly

208 Celano, *First Life*, 468–471.

honors, reverence, or vain praise. Indeed, they rejoiced at injuries and were saddened by honors. And so they went through the world as pilgrims and strangers, carrying nothing with them except Christ crucified. And because they were of the true vine, that is, Christ, they produced great and good fruits in souls that they won for God.[209]

Francis certainly wanted to be conformed in everything to Christ crucified, who, poor, suffering, and naked, remained hanging on the cross. For this reason, at the beginning of his conversion, he remained naked before the bishop; for this reason, at the end of his life, he wanted to leave the world naked; and he enjoined the friars who were around him in obedience of charity that, after his death, they should leave him naked there on the ground for the length of time necessary to travel a mile comfortably.[210]

How Francis, the friend of the bridegroom Jesus, tried to conform himself to Jesus himself in the fervor of charity and in the desire for the salvation of his brothers is shown clearly by this fact: that from the beginning of his conversion until the end, he always grew, like fire, in the ardor of love for Jesus. Driven

209 *The Little Flowers*, 1833.

210 Bonaventure, *Major Legend*, 1240.

by the Holy Spirit, he always inflamed the hearth of his heart, and therefore, as soon as he heard the love of God mentioned, he was so moved, impressed, and inflamed that he seemed to continually invoke with the bride of the Song of Songs, "Strengthen me with raisin cakes, refresh me with apples, for I am sick with love" (Sg 2:5). And he rekindled this love of his through all creatures.

In beautiful things he saw Him Who is the most beautiful. In weak things [he saw] the infirmities that the pious Jesus endured for our salvation, making himself a ladder of everything to reach the Beloved. Moreover, he was continually transformed with such singularity of love into the crucified Christ that he deserved to be configured not only in mind but also in body to the image of the Crucified. The zeal for eternal salvation gnawed at his insides to the point that he did not consider himself a friend of Christ if he did not set the souls redeemed by him on fire with love—hence, his battles in prayer, his labors in preaching, and his extraordinary commitment to giving good example.[211]

Christ Jesus crucified dwelt permanently in the depths of his spirit like a bag of myrrh placed on his

---

211 Alberto of Casale, *Tree of Life*, 2076–2077.

heart. He desired to be transformed completely in him by the excess and fire of love. As a pledge of singular devotion to him, beginning with the feast of the Epiphany for forty continuous days, that is, for the entire time in which Christ remained hidden in the desert, he withdrew into solitude, and secluded in his cell, reducing food and drink to the minimum possible, he devoted himself without interruption to fasting, prayers, and the praises of God.[212]

Christ Jesus, our Savior, appeared to him and said, "Francis, follow Me and in the footsteps of My poor and humble life. The fulfillment of every promise and every achievement of grace and glory is to configure and assimilate oneself to Me in feelings, intellect, and affections. If you adhere to Me with all your heart, with all your soul, mind, and strength so that every thought of yours is in Me or of Me, all your words are borrowed from Me or for Me or in My presence, and if all your actions are always for Me and to the honor and glory of My name, you will be My servant, and I will be with you and will speak through your mouth. Then, whoever listens to you will listen to Me; whoever welcomes you will welcome Me; whoever blesses you will

212 Bonaventure, *Major Legend*, 1163.

be blessed; and whoever curses you will be cursed" (see Mt 10:40; Gn 27:29; Nm 24:9)[213]

The Reception of the Stigmata

The Lord wished to show to the whole world the burning love and incessant memory of the Passion of Christ that he hid in his heart by means of the stupendous prerogative of an exceptional privilege with which He decorated him in the flesh while he was still alive.[214]

September AD 1224

Francis goes up to Mount La Verna to pray in honor of St. Michael; he opens the Gospel, which confirms the Passion.

Two years before he gave up his spirit to God, after many and varied labors, divine Providence took him aside and led him to a high mountain called Mount Verna. Here Francis began, according to his custom, to fast during [the] Lent in honor of St. Michael the Archangel, when he began to feel inundated with an extraordinary sweetness in contemplation, inflamed

213 Angelo Clareno, *Book of Tribulations*, 2124.

214 *Legend of the Three Companions*, 1483.

by a more vivid flame of heavenly desires, and filled with richer divine gifts. He rose to those heights not as an importunate scrutinizer of the majesty, who is oppressed by glory, but as a faithful and prudent servant, intent on seeking the will of God, to whom he desired with the greatest ardor to conform in all and for all.

He, therefore, knew from a divine voice that, at the opening of the Gospel, Christ would reveal to him what most pleased God in him and from him. After praying very devoutly, he took the sacred book of the Gospels from the altar and had it opened by his devout and holy companion in the name of the Holy Trinity. Having opened the book three times, he continuously came across the Passion of the Lord. Then the man filled with God understood that, as he had imitated Christ in the actions of his life, so he must be conformed to him in the sufferings and pains of the Passion before passing from this world.[215]

---

215 Bonaventure, *Major Legend*, 1223–1224.

The Feast of the Holy Cross, AD 1224

Francis prays to know the pain Christ felt on the cross and the love he had for all humanity.

The following day came, that is, the Feast of the Most Holy Cross, and Saint Francis, early in the morning before daybreak, threw himself in prayer before the door of his cell, turning his face toward the east, and he prayed in this way, "O my Lord Jesus Christ, I beg you to grant me two graces before I die: the first, that in my life I may feel in my soul and body, as much as possible, that pain that you, sweet Jesus, endured in the hour of your most bitter Passion. The second is that I may feel in my heart, as much as possible, that excessive love with which you, Son of God, were inflamed to willingly endure such a great Passion for us sinners." And remaining in this prayer for a long time, he understood that God would hear him and that, as far as was possible for a mere creature, he would be granted to feel the aforementioned things. In short, having made this promise, Saint Francis began to contemplate most devoutly the Passion of Christ and his infinite charity. And the fervor of devotion increased in him so much that he was completely transformed into Jesus, both by love and by compassion.[216]

September 17, AD 1224

Francis receives the stigmata.

[Then], he had a vision from God. A man appeared to him in the form of a Seraph, with wings hovering above him, with his hands outstretched, and with his feet together as if nailed to a cross. Two wings extended above his head, two spread out for flying, and two covered his whole body.

At that apparition, the blessed servant of the Most High felt filled with infinite admiration, though he could not understand its meaning. He was also filled with lively joy and overflowing happiness for the beautiful and sweet gaze, of an unimaginable beauty, with which the Seraph looked at him, but at the same time, he was terrified to see him nailed to the cross in the bitter pain of the Passion. He arose, so to speak, sad and happy, because joy and bitterness alternated in his spirit. He sought with ardor to discover the meaning of the vision, and for this his spirit was completely agitated.

---

216 *The Little Flowers*, 1919.

While he was in this state of worry and total uncertainty, behold: on his hands and feet began to appear the same marks of the nails that he had just seen on that mysterious crucified man. His hands and feet appeared to be pierced in the middle by nails, the heads of which were visible in the palms of the hands and on the backs of the feet, while the points protruded from the opposite sides. Those marks were round on the inside of the hands and elongated on the outside and formed almost a fleshy excrescence, as if they were the points of nails bent and hammered back. Likewise, on his feet were imprinted the marks of the nails protruding from the rest of the flesh. His right side was also pierced as if by a spear with a wide scar and often bled, wetting his tunic and undergarments with that sacred blood.[217]

Thus, the true love of Christ had transformed the lover into the very image of the Beloved.[218]

The man filled with God realized that the stigmata so clearly imprinted on his flesh could not remain hidden from his closest companions. Nevertheless, he feared to make the sacrament of the Lord known to the public and was torn by a great doubt: whether to say what he had seen or to remain silent. Finally, spurred

---

217 Celano, *First Life*, 484–485.

218 Bonaventure, *Major Legend*, 1228.

by the movement of his conscience, he related to some of those brothers closest to him, with great fear, the course of the vision we have related. Yet, the one who had appeared to him, he added, had told him some things that he would never reveal to anyone as long as he lived.

After the true love of Christ had transformed the lover into the perfect image of the Beloved, the number of forty days was completed that he had decided to spend on that mountain of solitude, and the Feast of the archangel Michael concluded, the angelic man, Francis, came down from the mountain. He carried with him the image of the Crucified, not depicted on tablets of stone or wood by the hand of an artisan, but written in the members of his flesh by the finger of the living God.

The holy and humble man strove with all diligence to conceal those sacred seals. Nevertheless, it pleased the Lord, for His own glory, to show through them some evident wonders so that their hidden power might be revealed clearly by clear signs and He might shine like a most brilliant star in the dense darkness of the dark age.[219]

---

219 Bonaventure, *Minor Legend*, 1377–1378.

The stigmata were in a certain sense the bull of the supreme pontiff Christ, who confirmed the Rule in all respects and in all things praised its author.[220]

October AD 1226

Upon Francis's death, Br. Elias of Cortona writes a letter to the friars in which he describes the stigmata in detail.

And now I bring you news of a great joy, a wondrous miracle. Never has such a portent been heard in the world except in the Son of God, who is Christ the Lord. Sometime before his death, our brother and father [Francis] appeared crucified, bearing imprinted on his body the five wounds that are truly the stigmata of Christ. His hands and feet were pierced as if by nails protruded from both sides, and they had scars the black color of the nails. His side appeared to be pierced by a lance, and he often emitted drops of blood.[221]

220 Bonaventure, *Major Legend*, 1085.

221 Elias of Cortona, *Letter on the Passing of St. Francis*, 309.

At La Verna, Francis consoles Brother Leo with a written blessing. (The parchment is conserved at the Basilica of St. Francis in Assisi.)

While the saint was locked in his cell on Mount Verna, a brother ardently desired to have for his consolation a written document containing the words of the Lord with brief notes written by Saint Francis. He was convinced that he could overcome or at least bear more easily a grave temptation—not of the flesh but of the spirit—that he felt oppressing him. Although he had a very strong desire, he did not dare confide in the most holy father. But what the creature did not tell [Francis], the Spirit revealed.

One day Francis called him and said, "Bring me paper and an inkwell, because I wish to write words and praises of the Lord, as I have meditated on them in my heart." Immediately, [Brother Leo] brought Francis what he had asked for. Then Francis, with his own hand, wrote the Praises of God and the words that he had in mind. At the end, he added a blessing for the friar. He said to him, "Take this little piece of paper and keep it carefully until the day of your death." He was then immediately freed from all temptation, and the writing, which has been preserved, has since worked wondrous things.

The Blessing to Brother Leo

The Lord bless you and keep you;
may he show you his face and have mercy on you.
May he turn his face toward you and give you peace.
(See Nm 6:24–26).

The Praises of God Most High

You are holy, Lord, the only God, You do wonders.
You are strong, You are great, You are the most high,
You are the almighty King.
You, Holy Father, the King of Heaven and earth.
You are Three and One, Lord God of gods;
You are good, all good, the highest good,
Lord, God, living and true.
You are love, charity.
You are wisdom; You are humility;
You are patience;
You are beauty; You are meekness; You are security;
You are inner peace; You are joy;
You are our hope and joy;
You are justice; You are moderation,
You are all our riches.
You are beauty, You are meekness;
You are the protector,
You are the guardian and defender;

You are strength; You are refreshment.
You are our hope, You are our faith,
You are our charity,
You are all our sweetness,
You are our eternal life:
Great and wonderful Lord,
God almighty, Merciful Savior.[222]

October–November AD 1224

Francis returns from La Verna to Assisi, working miracles.

Then Saint Francis came down from the mountain. Because the fame of his sanctity had already spread throughout the land among shepherds who had seen Mount La Verna totally ablaze, which was [seen as] a sign of some great miracle that God had done for Saint Francis, the people heard that he was passing through the roadways, and they came to see him. Men and women of low and high lineage, all with great devotion and desire, tried to touch him and kiss his hands. He would not deny that devotion to the people, although he had bandaged his palms to

222 Celano, *Second Life*, 632.

hide the sacred and holy stigmata. He also covered them with his sleeves and only offered the uncovered fingers to kiss. Although he strived to conceal the sacrament of the glorious stigmata to avoid every cause of worldly glory, it pleased God for his glory to reveal many miracles by virtue of the said sacred, holy, and glorious stigmata—especially on that journey from Mount La Verna to St. Mary of the Angels, and then many more in different parts of the world, during his life and after his death, so that their hidden and marvelous virtue and the excessive charity and mercy of Christ toward him, to whom he had marvelously given them, might be manifested to the world by clear and evident miracles.[223]

We have, indeed, seen these things that we narrate. With the hands with which we write, we have touched them, and what we testify with our lips, we have seen with aroused eyes, confirming for all time what we swore only once by touching the sacred objects. Many friars with us, while the Saint was alive, saw the same thing; at his death, then more than fifty friars, with countless laypeople, venerated him. Let there be no uncertainty; let no doubt arise regarding the gift of

---

223 *The Little Flowers*, 1926.

this eternal goodness! And may God grant that, through such seraphic love, many members adhere to the head, Christ, and that in such warfare they find themselves worthy of such armor, and that in the Kingdom they are raised to a similar order! Who in his right mind would not say that this belongs to the glory of Christ?[224]

Now nailed in flesh and spirit with Christ on the cross, Francis not only burned with seraphic love for God, he felt the same thirst as Christ crucified for the salvation of men. And since he could not walk because of the nails protruding from his feet, he had his half-dead body carried around towns and villages to encourage all others to carry the cross of Christ.

He said to the brothers, "Let us begin, brothers, to serve the Lord our God, because up to now we have accomplished little." He burned with a great desire to return to the humility of the beginning—to serve, as at the beginning, lepers and to recall his body, now worn out by fatigue, to the original willingness to service. With Christ as his leader, he [still] intended to do great things. And while his members were failing, he dreamed—strong and fervent in spirit—of

224 Celano, *Treatise of Miracles*, 830–831.

renewing the battle and triumphing over the enemy. In fact, there is no room for infirmity or for idleness when the impetus of love urges one to ever greater enterprises.[225]

225 Bonaventure, *Major Legend*, 1237.

The Transitus

October AD 1224

Brother Elias prophesies that Francis has two years to live.

Almost twenty years had now passed since his conversion, as had been communicated to him by divine will. And it happened in this way. While blessed Francis and Brother Elias were in Foligno, at night, a priest of very advanced age and of venerable appearance, dressed in white, appeared to Brother Elias in a dream and said to him, "Go, brother, and tell Francis that, since eighteen years have passed since he renounced the world to follow Christ, he has only two years left in this life. Then the Lord will call him to Himself in the world of the multitude."[226]

226 Celano, *First Life*, 508.

March AD 1225

Francis is afflicted with an eye disease. Bishop Hugolino and Brother Elias insist he undergo treatment.

When the bishop of Ostia [Hugolino], who later became pope [Gregory IX], realized that blessed Francis had been and continued to be so harsh on his body, and especially that he was beginning to lose his eyesight and refused to be treated, inspired by much mercy and compassion for him, he admonished him in the following way: "Brother, you do not do well to refuse to have your eyes treated, because your health and your life are very useful to you and to others. If you have so much compassion for your sick brothers and have always cared for them, you should not be cruel to yourself during this grave and evident need of yours. Therefore, I order you to allow yourself to be aided and treated."

Two years before he died, when he was already seriously ill and especially suffering from eye problems, he lived at San Damiano in a little cell made of mats. The minister general, seeing him suffer so much from the eye disease, ordered him to be helped and treated. He even added that he wanted to be present personally when the doctor began the treatment so as to be more certain of the matter and also to comfort him, since he was in so much pain. But it was very cold then, and the season was not favorable to begin the treatment.[227]

April–May AD 1225

In San Damiano, Francis receives the promise of eternal life and dictates the Canticle of the Creatures.

Being so tormented by so many afflictions, one night, moved to piety for himself, Francis said, "Lord, come to my aid, look upon my infirmities, so that I may know how to bear them patiently!"

And immediately it was said to him in spirit, "Tell Me, brother: if someone, for these tribulations and infirmities of yours, were to give you a treasure so great and precious that the whole world would be as nothing in comparison, would you not be happy?"

Francis answered, "Lord, such a treasure would truly be great and precious, wondrous and desirable."

Then he heard that voice again, "Therefore, brother, be joyful and happy in your illnesses and tribulations. And from now on, live assuredly, as if you were already in possession of My Kingdom." [. . .]

---

227 *Legend of Perugia/Assisi Compilation*, 1590.

Francis sat down and thought for a while. Then began to sing the praises of God for His creatures. [. . .]

Most High, all-powerful, good Lord,
Yours are the praises, the glory, and
the honor. and all blessing.
To You alone, Most High, do they belong,
and no human is worthy to mention Your name.
Praised be You, my Lord, with all Your crea-
tures, especially Messer Brother Sun,
Who is the day, and through whom You give us light.
And he is beautiful and radiant with great splendor;
and bears a likeness of You, Most High One.
Praised be You, my Lord, through Sister Moon
and the stars in Heaven
You formed them clear and precious and beautiful.
Praised be You, my Lord, through Brother Wind,
and through the air, cloudy and serene,
and every kind of weather,
through whom You give sustenance to Your creatures.
Praised be You, my Lord, through Sister Water,
who is very useful and hum-
ble and precious and chaste.
Praised be You, my Lord, through Brother Fire,
through whom You light the night,

and he is beautiful and playful and robust and strong.
Praised be You, my Lord, through
our Sister Mother Earth,
who sustains and governs us,
and who produces various fruit with
colored flowers and herbs.
Praised be You, my Lord, through
our Sister Bodily Death,
from whom no one living can escape.
Woe to those who die in mortal sin.
Blessed are those whom death will
find in Your most holy will,
for the second death shall do them no harm.
Praise and bless my Lord and give Him thanks
and serve Him with great humility.[228]

June AD 1225

Francis adds a verse on forgiveness to the Canticle, which leads to the reconciliation between the bishop and mayor of Assisi.

At that same time, while he was lying ill [in San Damiano], having already composed and sung the

228 *Mirror of Perfection,* 1799; 1819–1820.

Praises, it happened that the bishop of Assisi, who was then in office, excommunicated the podestà [that is, the mayor] of the city. The latter, enraged, by way of retaliation, had this harsh proclamation announced: that no one should sell to the bishop, buy anything from him, or make contracts with him. [It escalated] to such a point that they came to hate one another.

Francis, sick as he was, was moved with mercy for them, especially because no ecclesiastic or layperson was interested in reestablishing peace and harmony between the two. So he said to his companions, "It is a great shame for us, servants of God, that the bishop and the podestà hate each other so much and no one takes the trouble to restore peace and harmony between them." He then composed this stanza, to be added to the Praises:

Praised be You, my Lord, through those who give pardon for Your love and bear infirmity and tribulation. Blessed are those who endure in peace, for by You, Most High, shall they be crowned.

Then he called one of his companions and said to him, "Go and tell the podestà on my behalf to come to the vescovado [that is, the bishop's residence], together with the magnates of the city and others whom he can bring with him." The friar went away, and the Saint said to the other two companions, "Go and sing the Canticle of Brother Sun in the presence of the bishop and the podestà and the others who are present there. I trust in the Lord that he will humble their hearts, and they will make peace and return to their former friendship and affection." [. . .]

After the Canticle was finished, the podestà said before all those present, "I tell you in truth that I would be willing to forgive not only the bishop, whom I must consider my lord, but also anyone who should murder my brother or son." Then he threw himself at the bishop's feet, saying to him, "For the love of our Lord Jesus Christ and of his servant Francis, behold, I am ready to satisfy you in everything, as you please."

The bishop took him in his arms, stood up, and replied, "For the office I hold, I should be humble. Unfortunately, I have a temperament prone to anger. I beg you to forgive me." And so the two embraced and kissed one another with great cordiality and affection.[229]

---

229 *Legend of Perugia/Assisi Compilation*, 1616.

July–August AD 1225

Francis goes to Rieti, where he undergoes a crude procedure on his eyes.

The doctors advised him, and the brothers insistently urged him, to consent to having his eyes treated by cauterization. The man of God humbly agreed, believing that the operation was both healthy and painful at the same time. They called the surgeon, who came and immersed the iron instrument for cauterization in the fire.

But the servant of Christ, comforting his already shaken and horrified body, began to speak to the fire as if to a friend. He said, "O my brother fire, the Most High has created you splendid and enviable by all other creatures, strong, beautiful, and useful. At this moment, be good to me and kind. I pray to the great Lord who created you to moderate your heat for me. Thus, you will burn gently, and I will be able to bear you." Having finished the prayer, he traced the sign of the cross on the now red-hot iron and stood there waiting fearlessly.

The iron sank crackling into his tender flesh, while the cauterization was extended from the ear to the eyebrow. Though the pain that the fire inflicted was intense, the Saint declared to his brothers, "Praised be the Most High, because I tell the truth, I felt neither the heat of the fire nor any pain in my flesh." And turning to the doctor, "If the flesh is not yet well-cooked, dig in it again."

That experienced doctor, admiring that sublime strength of spirit in that weak flesh as if it were a divine miracle, exclaimed, "O brothers, I tell you that today I have seen wonders."[230]

April–June AD 1226

Francis goes to Siena, where he becomes very sick; there, he writes a short Testament.

Six months before his death, while staying in Siena for the treatment of his eyes, he became seriously ill throughout his body. Following the rupture of blood vessels in his stomach due to the dysfunction of his liver, he suffered an abundant loss of blood, so much so that he feared his end was imminent.[231]

One evening, blessed Francis was seized by retching because of his stomach disease. And in the violent effort it took to retch, he vomited up blood. And this took place throughout the night until morning. His

230 Bonaventure, *Major Legend*, 1097.

231 Celano, *First Life*, 502.

companions, seeing him at the point of death from exhaustion and the pain caused by the disease, with great sorrow and outpouring of tears, said to him, "Father, what shall we do? Bless us and all your other brothers. And leave to your brothers a testament of your will, so that, if the Lord wants to call you from this world, they can always keep in mind and repeat: 'Our father, on the point of dying, left these words to his brothers and sons.'" He then said, "Call Brother Benedetto of Piratro to me." He was a priest friar, a discreet and holy man, who had been in the Order for a long time. And he sometimes celebrated Mass in that same cell for blessed Francis, since the latter, although sick, when it was possible, always and willingly wanted to listen devoutly to the Mass.[232]

April–May AD 1226

[When he came to him, blessed Francis said:] "Write that I bless all my brothers who are now in this Religion and those who will enter it until the end of the world. And since, because of weakness and the suffering of illness, I cannot speak, I briefly manifest to my

232 *Legend of Perugia/Assisi Compilation*, 1587.

brothers my will in these three words. That is: in sign and memory of my blessing and my testament, always love one another, always love and observe our lady holy poverty, and always be faithful and submissive to the prelates and all the clerics of holy mother Church."[233]

Francis goes to Cortona.

Upon hearing this news [that Francis was so sick], Brother Elias came quickly from afar. When he arrived, Francis improved to the point that he was able to leave Siena and go with him to the Cells [Italian: *Le Celle*] near Cortona. But after a few days of arriving, the illness took hold again. His stomach swelled, his legs and feet became swollen, and his stomach worsened such that it was almost impossible to retain any food. He then asked Brother Elias to please have him taken back to Assisi.[234]

Francis asks his body for forgiveness
for having treated it so poorly.

Francis, herald of God, walked the paths of Christ through many pains and grave illnesses, and he did not

233 St. Francis, *The Testament of Siena*, 132–135.

234 Celano, *First Life*, 502.

withdraw his foot until he crowned the good beginning with an even holier end. In fact, although he was deprived of strength and his body was completely ruined, he never paused in his race towards perfection; he never allowed the rigor of discipline to be softened. So much so that even when his body was exhausted, he did not feel like showing it any consideration without remorse of conscience.

One day, even against his will, having to soothe the sufferings of his body with various medicines because the pain was beyond his strength, he turned with confidence to a friar because he knew that he would give him wise counsel. "What do you think, dearest son, of the fact that my conscience often reproaches me for the [lack of] care with which I treat my body? Perhaps it fears that I am being too indulgent because it is sick and that I am trying to help it with rare medicines. Not that the body takes pleasure in anything, because ruined as it is by a long illness, it has lost all taste."

[After a dialogue, Francis] turned to his body and began to say to it joyfully, "Rejoice, brother body, and forgive me: behold, now I am ready to satisfy your desires; I willingly prepare to listen to your complaints!" But what could have brought comfort to that poor, almost extinct body? What could have been offered to support it, since it was ruined in every part? Francis was already dead to this world, but Christ lived in him. The delights of the world were a cross for him because he bore the Cross of Christ rooted in his heart. And precisely for this reason the stigmata shone outwardly in the flesh, because within, their root extended very deeply into his soul.[235]

September AD 1226

Francis returns to Assisi.

Having just returned from the hermitage in Bagnara, Francis was seriously ill and lying in the episcopal palace of Assisi. The inhabitants of the city feared that if the Saint were to die at night, the friars would secretly remove his body and bring it to another city. So they decided that guards should carefully keep guard each night outside and all around the walls of the palace.

Given his serious conditions, and to comfort his spirit so that it would not fail because of his harsh and various infirmities, Francis often had his companions sing by day the Praises of the Lord that he himself had composed earlier during his illness. He also had them

---

235 Celano, *Second Life*, 800–801; 211.

sung at night to give some relief to the guards who kept watch over him outside the palace.

Brother Elias saw that Francis, amidst such atrocious suffering, drew courage and joy in the Lord from singing and observed, "Dearest brother, I am very edified and consoled by the joy that you feel and show to your companions during this harsh suffering and illness. The inhabitants of this city certainly venerate you as a saint in life and in death. However, since they are convinced that you are about to die from this great and incurable illness, when hearing these Praises resound, they might think or say to themselves, 'How is it possible that someone so close to death would express such lively joy? He would do better to think about death!'"

Francis answered him, "Do you remember the vision you had near Foligno? You told me then that it had been revealed that I had only two years to live. Well, even before you had that vision, by the grace of the Holy Spirit, who suggests to the hearts of his faithful all good things and puts them on their lips, I often thought about my end, day and night. But from the hour that that revelation was communicated to you, I have been concerned each day with preparing myself for death."

In a fit of fervor, he then continued, "Brother, let me rejoice in the Lord and in his praises in the midst of my sorrows, because, by the grace of the Holy Spirit, I am so closely united to my Lord that, by his mercy, I can well exult in the Most High!"[236]

September AD 1226

Shortly before his death, Francis writes his final Testament. Pope Gregory refers to it in a papal bull, Quo elongati.

All the more so since the blessed confessor of Christ, Francis, of holy memory, not wanting his Rule to be subjected to explanation through the interpretation of any friar, near the end of his life commanded—and this command is called his *Testament*—that no gloss (explanatory comments) should be made on the words of the Rule itself, and that it should not be said, to use his words, that they should be understood thus or in such a way, adding that the friars should not ask for letters from the Apostolic See, and he also put in other directives that could not be observed without considerable difficulty.. For these reasons, uncertain whether

236 *Legend of Perugia/Assisi Compilation*, 1637.

you are bound to the observance of the said Testament, you have asked Us to remove this doubt from your conscience and that of the other friars by Our authority.[237]

The Testament

The Lord gave me, Brother Francis, thus, to begin doing penance in this way: for when I was in sin, it seemed too bitter for me to see lepers. And the Lord Himself led me among them, and I showed mercy to them. And when I left them, what had seemed bitter to me was turned into sweetness of soul and body. And afterwards I delayed a little and left the world.

And the Lord gave me such faith in churches that I would pray with simplicity in this way and say: "We adore You, Lord Jesus Christ, in all Your churches throughout the whole world and we bless You because by Your holy cross You have redeemed the world."

Afterwards the Lord gave me, and gives me still, such faith in priests who live according to the rite of the holy Roman Church because of their orders that, were they to persecute me, I would still want to have recourse to them. And if I had as much wisdom as

237 Gregory IX, Bull *Quo elongati*, 2729.

Solomon and found impoverished priests of this world, I would not preach in their parishes against their will.

And I desire to respect, love, and honor them and all others as my lords. And I do not want to consider any sin in them, because I discern the Son of God in them and they are my lords. And I act in this way because, in this world, I see nothing corporally of the Most High Son of God except His Most Holy Body and Blood, which they receive and they alone administer to others. I want to have these most holy mysteries honored and venerated above all things, and I want to reserve them in precious places.

Wherever I find our Lord's most holy Name and written Word in unbecoming places, I want to gather them up, and I beg that they be gathered up and placed in a becoming place. And we must honor all theologians and those who minister the most holy divine Word and respect them as those who minister to us spirit and life.

And after the Lord gave me some brothers, no one showed me what I had to do, but the Most High Himself revealed to me that I should live according to the pattern of the Holy Gospel. And I had this written down simply and in a few words and the Lord Pope confirmed it for me. And those who came to receive life gave whatever they had to the poor and were content with one tunic, patched inside and out, with a cord, and short trousers.

We desired nothing more. We clerical [brothers] said the Office as other clerics did; the lay brothers said the Our Father; and we quite willingly remained in churches. And we were simple and subject to all.

And I worked with my hands, and I still desire to work; and I earnestly desire all brothers to give themselves to honest work. Let those who do not know how to work learn, not from desire to receive wages, but for example and to avoid idleness. And when we are not paid for our work, let us have recourse to the table of the Lord, begging alms from door to door.

The Lord revealed a greeting to me that we should say: "May the Lord give you peace." Let the brothers be careful not to receive in any way churches or poor dwellings or anything else built for them unless they are according to the holy poverty we have promised in the Rule. As pilgrims and strangers, let them always be guests there.

I strictly command all the brothers through obedience, wherever they may be, not to dare to ask any letter from the Roman Curia, either personally or through an intermediary, whether for a church or another place or under the pretext of preaching or the persecution of their bodies. But wherever they have not been received, let them flee into another country to do penance with the blessing of God.

And I firmly wish to obey the minister general of this fraternity and the other guardian whom it pleases him to give me. And I so wish to be a captive in his hands that I cannot go anywhere or do anything beyond obedience and his will, for he is my master. And although I may be simple and infirm, I nevertheless want to have a cleric always with me who will celebrate the Office for me as it is prescribed in the Rule.

And let all the brothers be bound to obey their guardians and to recite the Office according to the Rule. And if some might have been found who are not reciting the Office according to the Rule and want to change it in some way, or who are not Catholics, let all the brothers, wherever they may have found one of them, be bound through obedience to bring him before the custodian of that place nearest to where they found him.

And let the custodian be strictly bound through obedience to keep him securely day and night as a man in chains so that he cannot be taken from his hands until he can personally deliver him into the hands of his minister. And let the minister be bound through obedience to send him with such brothers who would guard him as a prisoner until they deliver him to the Lord of Ostia, who is the Lord, the Protector, and the Corrector of this fraternity. And the brothers may not say: "This is another Rule."

Because this is a remembrance, admonition, exhortation, and my testament, which I, little brother Francis, make for you, my blessed brothers, that we might observe the Rule we have promised in a more Catholic way.

And let the minister general and all the other ministers and custodians be bound through obedience not to add to or take away from these words. And let them always have this writing with them together with the Rule. And in all the chapters that they hold, when they read the Rule, let them also read these words. And I strictly command all my cleric and lay brothers, through obedience, not to place any gloss upon the Rule or upon these words saying: "They should be understood in this way." But as the Lord has given me to speak and write the Rule and these words simply and purely, may you understand them simply and without gloss and observe them with a holy activity until the end.

And whoever observes these things, let him be blessed in Heaven with the blessing of the Most High Father, and on earth with the blessing of His Beloved Son with the Most Holy Spirit, the Paraclete, and all the powers of Heaven and with all the saints.

And, as far as I can, I, little brother Francis, your servant, confirm for you, both within and without, this most holy blessing. (Amen).[238]

Early October 1226

Sensing that death is near, Francis is taken to the Portiuncula. Along the way, he stops to bless the city.

Francis was carried to the Portiuncula on a stretcher, since he could not ride due to the worsening of his illness. When the brothers who were carrying him reached the hospital, he told them to put the stretcher on the ground and turn him so that he was facing the city of Assisi. In fact, he had almost completely lost his eyesight because of the very serious and long-standing disease of his eyes. He straightened up a little on the stretcher and blessed Assisi with these words, "Lord, I believe that this city was formerly a refuge and abode of

238 St. Francis of Assisi, *The Testament*, 110–131.

wicked, iniquitous men, ill-famed in all these regions. But by your abundant mercy, in the time that pleased you, I see that you have shown the superabundance of your goodness, so that the city has become a refuge and abode for those who know you and give glory to your name and spread the fragrance of holy life, correct doctrine, and good fame throughout the Christian people. I beg you, therefore, O Lord Jesus Christ, Father of mercies, not to look upon our ingratitude but to remember only the abundance of your goodness that you have shown here. May this city always be the land and habitation of those who know you and glorify your blessed and glorious name forever and ever. Amen." After he said this prayer, he was transported to Our Lady of the Portiuncula.[239]

Francis blesses Brother Bernard.

[Once in St. Mary of the Angels,] he then turned to a companion and said to him, "Go tell Brother Bernard to come to me immediately." He left immediately and brought him to Francis. [. . .] Bernard came up to him, and Francis placed his hand on his head and blessed him. Then he spoke to one of his companions, "Write

239 *Legend of Perugia/Assisi Compilation*, 1655.

what I am about to say. The first brother given to me by the Lord was Bernard. He was the first to embrace and achieve the perfection of the Gospel, distributing all he had to the poor. For this and for his many merits, I am bound to love him more than any other brother of the Order. I therefore desire and command, as far as it lies in my power, that whoever is the minister general should love and honor him as he would me, and that the ministers provincial and all the friars of the Order should consider him as another myself." These words were a source of great consolation for Bernard and the friars present.[240]

Lady Jacopa, a Roman noblewoman and benefactor, is allowed to see Francis.

Jacopa dei Settesoli, whose fame in the city of Rome was equal to her sanctity, had merited the privilege of a special affection from the Saint. It is not for me to repeat, in praise of her, her illustrious lineage, nobility, great wealth, and finally the marvelous perfection of her virtues and her long chastity as a widow. Therefore, when the Saint was ill with that disease that would lead him, after so much suffering, to a blessed death and the

240 *Legend of Perugia/Assisi Compilation*, 1664.

happy completion of his life, a few days before dying, he asked that Lady Jacopa be notified in Rome so that, if she wanted to see the one whom she loved so much as an exile on earth and who was now close to returning to his homeland, she should come quickly. A letter was written, a very fast messenger was sought, and when he was found, he prepared for the journey. Suddenly, the trampling of horses, the din of soldiers, and the noise of a contingent were heard at the door. One of the brothers—the one who was giving instructions to the messenger—approached the door and found himself in the presence of the one he was looking for far away. Amazed, he quickly approached the Saint and full of joy said, "Father, I bring you good news." The Saint, anticipating him, answered, "Blessed be God, who has brought Lady Jacopa, our 'brother,' to us! Open the doors and let her come in, since for Brother Jacopa the decree regarding women is not to be observed!"[241]

Francis's final moments.

While the brothers were shedding bitter tears and lamenting in desolation, he had bread brought to him. He blessed it, broke it, and gave a little piece to each of

241 Celano, *Treatise of Miracles*, 860.

them to eat. He then asked for the book containing the Gospels, and he requested that the Gospel of John be read, beginning with the passage, "Before the feast of Passover . . ." (Jn 13:1). He was recalling the most holy supper at that moment, which the Lord had celebrated with his disciples the final time. And Francis did all this precisely in venerable memory of that supper and to show how much tender love he had for the brothers.

He spent the few days that remained in a hymn of praise, and he invited his dearly beloved companions to praise Christ with him. Then, as best he could, he broke out into this psalm, "With my own voice I cry to the LORD; with my own voice I beseech the LORD" (Ps 141(142):2). He then invited all creatures to praise God, and he exhorted them to divine love with certain verses that he had composed. He exhorted even death—terrible and odious to all—to praise [the Lord], and going to meet her joyfully, he invited her to be his guest, saying, "Welcome, sister death!"

He then turned to the doctor. He said, "Courage, brother doctor, tell me that death is imminent: for me it will be the door of life!" Then, to the brothers, he said, "When you see me reduced *in extremis*, lay me naked on the ground as you saw me the day before yesterday. And after I am dead, let me lie like that for the time necessary to walk one mile comfortably."[242]

Lying thus stripped in the dust of the earth, the athlete of Christ covered with his left hand the wound in his right side, so that it would not be seen, and raising his serene face to Heaven, as was his wont, all intent on that glory, he began to magnify the Most High, because—freed from everything—he was now about to pass freely to Him.[243]

Then he said to the friars, "I have done my part; may Christ teach you yours."[244]

October 3–4, AD 1226

Francis dies on the night between October 3–4.

Since he would soon become earth and ashes, he wanted a sackcloth to be placed on him and ashes to be sprinkled over him. Then, while many brothers, of whom he was the father and leader, were gathered there with reverence and awaiting his blessed *transitus* and blessed end, his most holy soul was freed from the

242 Celano, *Second Life*, 808–810.

243 Bonaventure, *Minor Legend*, 1386.

244 Bonaventure, *Major Legend*, 1239.

flesh. He ascended into the eternal light, and his body fell asleep in the Lord. [245]

The larks, who are friends of the light and fear the darkness of the evening, at the moment of the passing of the Saint, even though night was already approaching, came in great flocks above the roof of the house. Circling for a long time with I know not what unusual jubilation, they bore joyful and open testimony to the glory of the Saint who had so often invited them to praise God.[246]

October 4, AD 1226

Francis's body is transported into Assisi.
On the way, the procession stops in San Damiano so St. Clare and the sisters can pay homage to him.

The next day at dawn, the citizens of Assisi arrived [at the Portiuncula] with all the clergy. Taking his sacred body, they honorably transported it to the city amidst hymns, songs, and trumpet blasts. Celebrating together the solemnity of those funereal liturgies, everyone equipped himself with olive branches and those of other trees and continued in procession, all

---

245 Celano, *First Life*, 512.

246 Bonaventure, *Major Legend*, 1245.

the while singing prayers and praises to the Lord in the splendor of innumerable candles. The children carried their father, and the flock followed its shepherd, who had preceded them to meet the universal Shepherd.

When they arrived at the place where he had founded the religious Order of the Sacred Virgins and Poor Ladies, they placed the sacred body in the church of San Damiano, where his beloved daughters, whom he had won for the Lord, lived. Then, the small grate was opened through which the handmaids of Christ received the Eucharist at the appointed times. The coffin was also opened, which contained that treasure of celestial virtues, now carried by a few, he who was accustomed to carrying many during his life.

And behold, Lady Clare—who was truly light for the richness of her merits [Editor: Clara, St. Clare's name in Latin, can be translated as "light"], the first mother of all the others, because she had been the first little plant of that religious family—comes with her daughters to see the father who no longer speaks to them and will no longer return to them, because he is going elsewhere.[247]

247 Celano, *First Life*, 523–524.

The friars then lifted the body of the Saint from the funeral stretcher and held him in [the sisters'] arms for a long time near that window, until Clare and her sisters were consoled, although they were all full of and worn out with grief and tears, seeing themselves deprived of the comforts and exhortations of such a father.[248]

[The procession] finally arrived in the city with great joy, and they reverently buried that precious treasure in the church of St. George. For, it was there where he had learned letters as a child, and it was there where he later preached the first time. Therefore, he rightly found there, at last, the first place of his rest.[249]

---

248 *Mirror of Perfection*, 1807–1808.

249 Bonaventure, *Major Legend*, 1250–1251.

Saint Francis of Assisi

Following Francis's death, word of his holiness and miracles spreads.

Buried near the city of Assisi, [Francis] began to shine everywhere through many and varied miracles, such that in a short time, he led a large part of the world to be amazed at the renewed age.[250]

Since the immense mercy of Christ the Lord confirms by the work of miracles how true are the things that have been written and diffused about His saint and our father Francis, and since it seems absurd to subject to human judgment what is approved by miracles, I, a humble son of the father [Francis], beg and ask all to receive the [following] miracles described with devotion and to listen to them with reverence.[251]

250 Celano, *Second Life*, 816.

251 Celano, *Treatise of Miracles*, 1019.

Celano begins narrating the miracles of St. Francis by referring to the birth and growth of the Franciscan Order.

In [this] first chapter of this narrative, in which we have undertaken to write of the miracles of our most holy father Francis, we believe it is proper to collocate, before anything else, that solemn prodigy by which it was as if the world were admonished, shaken, and terrorized. Such was precisely the birth of the Order—fruitfulness of the sterile woman, the begetting of a lineage with so many branches.[252]

Bonaventure begins his narration of the miracles of St. Francis by referring to the stigmata.

As I prepare to narrate, to the honor of almighty God and the glory of blessed father Francis, some of the approved miracles that occurred after his glorification in Heaven, I have judged it necessary to begin with the one that, better than any other, reveals the power of the cross of Jesus and renews its glory. The new man, Francis, shone through a new and stupendous miracle when, by an extraordinary privilege not granted in

252 Celano, *Treatise of Miracles*, 821.

previous ages, he appeared signed and adorned with the sacred stigmata, and he was configured, in this body of death, to the figure of the Crucified. Whatever praise the human tongue may utter of this prodigy can never be adequate.[253]

Following are some of the most widely circulated miracles attributed to St. Francis from the earliest time.

Francis appears to the pope in a dream, revealing his stigmata.

To dispel every cloud of doubt and to prove the authenticity of this stupendous and incontestable miracle [that is, the stigmata], there are not only testimonies, which are absolutely worthy of belief on account of those who saw and touched it, but also the admirable apparitions and wonders that shone after the death of the Saint.

Pope Gregory IX, of happy memory, to whom the Saint had prophesied his election to the chair of Peter, had doubts in his heart about the wound in [Francis's] side before canonizing the standard bearer of the cross. Well, one night, as the glorious prelate himself

253 Bonaventure, *Major Legend*, 1256.

recounted through tears, blessed Francis appeared to him in a dream and, with a rather severe face, rebuked him for his hesitations. Raising his right arm, he uncovered his wound and asked [the pope] for a vial to collect the flowing blood that was flowing from his side. In a vision, the Supreme Pontiff offered the sought-after vial and saw it fill to the brim with living blood. From that time on, he was inflamed with great devotion and fervent zeal for that sacred miracle, to the point that he could not bear it when anyone dared, through pride or presumption, to ignore the reality of those most brilliant stigmata without severely rebuking him.[254]

A deceased woman is resurrected through the intercession of St. Francis.

In the village of Monte Marano near Benevento, there was a woman of noble birth but even more nobility in virtue. She was especially devoted to Saint Francis, whom she served with deep devotion. Oppressed by illness and now at the end of her life, she followed the fate of every mortal. She died toward sunset, and her funeral was postponed until the following day in order to allow the large crowd of relatives to participate

254 Bonaventure, *Major Legend*, 1257.

in the sacred rite. At night, clerics arrived with psalters to sing the funeral rites and night vigils while the crowd stood all around.

Then, suddenly, in front of all, the woman sat up in her bed and called out to a priest from among those present, who was her godfather, saying, "I wish to confess, Father. Hear my sin! In fact, I am dead and was destined for a harsh imprisonment because I had not yet confessed a sin that I will now reveal to you." She added, "But since Saint Francis, to whom I was always very devoted, prayed for me, I was allowed to return to life in such a way that, having confessed that sin, I could merit pardon. And behold, before all of you, having confessed the sin, I will hasten to my promised rest." Then, after she confessed with fear and trembling to the amazed priest and received absolution, she lay down quietly on the bed and fell asleep happily in the Lord.[255]

St. Francis prays for the salvation of the soul of a knight.

Once, when blessed father Francis was in Celano to preach, a knight invited him to have a meal with him. At first, he refused and resisted his devout and repeated

---

255 Celano, *Treatise of Miracles*, 863.

prayers for a long time, though he finally let himself be persuaded by [the knight's] insistence. When the time for lunch arrived, a splendid table was laid out. The devout guest rejoiced, as well as his entire family, at the arrival of the poor friars.

Blessed Francis, remaining standing and raising his eyes to Heaven, called the guest to him and said, "Behold, brother guest, won over by your prayers, I have entered your house to eat. Now obey my warning immediately, for you will not eat here but in another place. Confess your sins with devotion and contrition, and let no sin remain in you that you do not confess. Today the Lord will reward you because you have so devoutly welcomed his poor friars."

The man was immediately convinced by the holy words, and he called a companion of Saint Francis, who was a priest, and revealed to him all his sins in a sincere confession. He then made arrangements for his household and awaited, without a shadow of a doubt, the word of the Saint to be fulfilled. Finally, they all sat down at the table and began to eat. After the knight made the sign of the cross, he stretched out his trembling hand towards the bread. But before he could withdraw it, he bowed his head and expired.[256]

In Catalonia, a man is healed by the apparition of Saint Francis.

In Catalonia, near Lerida, there was a man named John, who was a devotee of blessed Francis. One evening, he was walking along a road where there was an ambush lying in wait to kill not him, who had no enemies, but someone else, who resembled him and who was in his company that evening. Leaping from his hiding place, the assassin mistook John for his enemy and struck him several times with his sword. There was absolutely no hope of saving him. In fact, the first blow almost completely tore off one of his shoulders and arm, while a second opened such a gash beneath his breast that the breath that exhaled from it could have extinguished six candles at once.

[When the doctors arrived], it was their opinion that it was impossible to save him because the wounds were already purulent. In fact, they gave off an unbearable stench such that even his wife was repulsed by them. Having now lost all hope in human remedies,

256 Celano, *Treatise of Miracles*, 864.

the wounded man turned all his devotion to imploring the patronage of blessed father Francis, whom he had already invoked with great trust under the flurry of the blows, together with the Blessed Virgin. And behold, while he was languishing in the lonely bed of his misfortune, groaning and fading in and out of consciousness, he continued to repeat the name of Francis.

Then a man dressed as a Friar Minor, seemingly having entered through the window, approached him and called him by name, saying, "Because you have believed in me, behold, the Lord will heal you." The sick man asked him who he was, to which he replied that he was Saint Francis. He went to him, untied the bandages from his wounds, and spread an ointment (or so it seemed) over all his wounds. At the gentle touch of those stigmatized hands, which had received the power to heal from the Savior, the rottenness in his flesh disappeared, his skin was restored, and the wounds were healed. The wounded man was left completely healthy as before.[257]

---

257 Bonaventure, *Major Legend*, 1260.

Through Francis's intercession,
a child is brought back to life.

There was a little boy of just seven years old, who was the son of a notary in Rome. Like many children, he wished to accompany his mother, who happened to be going to the church of San Marco to hear a sermon. Instead, she sent him home. Embittered, the little boy was overwhelmed by an unknown diabolical instinct, and he threw himself from the window. Falling down with a final gasp, he died. The mother had not gone far when she heard the thud of his fallen body. Suspecting the tragedy of her treasure, she ran home quickly and saw her lifeless son.

Immediately, she dug her nails into her skin and yelled out bitterly to the neighbors. The doctors were summoned to the lifeless body in the hopes that they would be able to give life back to the dead child. But the prognosis was not good, and treatment was useless. The doctors could only explain but not remedy the fact, which was now in the hands of only God. As he was deprived of warmth and life, feeling, movement, and strength, the child was declared dead by the doctors.

Brother Rao, of the Order of Minors, was a very famous preacher in the city of Rome and had come there to preach. He approached the boy and, full of faith, said to the boy's father, "Do you believe that the Saint of God, Francis, can raise your son from the dead through the love that he always had for the Son of God, the Lord Jesus Christ?"

The father replied, "I firmly believe and confess this. I will be at his service forever and will publicly visit his holy [burial] place." The brother then knelt down with his companion and invited everyone present to pray. After the prayer, the boy began slowly to yawn, to raise his arms, and to stand up again. The mother ran up and embraced her son, while the father could not contain himself out of joy. The entire crowd, full of admiration, magnified Christ and his Saint with loud cries. From that moment the boy began to walk before everyone. He had been restored to life in excellent condition.[258]

March 19, AD 1227

Cardinal Hugolino is elected Pope Gregory IX.

When Pope Honorius III died, the bishop of Ostia [Cardinal Hugolino, the protector of the Franciscan Order] was elected supreme pontiff, taking the name

258 Celano, *Treatise of Miracles*, 865.

Gregory IX. Until the end of his life, he was an outstanding benefactor and defender of the friars, of all other religious, and especially of the poor of Christ. For this reason, we believe that he now belongs to the assembly of saints.[259]

July 16, AD 1228

Pope Gregory IX comes to Assisi to celebrate the canonization of Saint Francis.

The pastor of the Church [Pope Gregory IX], after recognizing with full faith and certainty the sanctity of Francis—not only from the miracles heard after his death but also from the proof seen with his own eyes and touched with his own hands during his life—rightly recognized and had not the slightest doubt that he was glorified in Heaven by the Lord. Therefore, he went personally to the city of Assisi, and on July 16 of the year 1228 of the Incarnation of the Lord, on a Sunday, with great solemnity—which would be too long to recount—enrolled the blessed father in the catalogue of the Saints.[260]

---

259 *Legend of the Three Companions*, 1481.

260 Bonaventure, *Major Legend*, 1252–1253.

With his hands raised toward Heaven, the blessed Pontiff [Gregory IX] with a thundering voice cries out and says, "To the praise and glory of almighty God, Father, Son, and Holy Spirit, and to the honor of the Roman Church, while We venerate on earth the most blessed father Francis, whom the Lord has glorified in Heaven, after having gathered the opinion of our brothers (the cardinals) and of the other prelates, We decree that his name be inscribed in the Catalogue of Saints and that his feast be celebrated on the day of his death."[261]

July 19, AD 1228

Pope Gregory confirms St. Francis's canonization in a papal bull.

"Therefore, since the wondrous events of his glorious life are quite well known to Us because of the great familiarity he had with Us while We still occupied a lower rank, and since We are fully convinced by reliable witnesses of the many brilliant miracles, We and the flock entrusted to Us, by the mercy of God, are confident of being assisted at his intercession and of having in Heaven a patron whose friendship We enjoyed on earth. With

261 Celano, *First Life*, 540.

the consultation and approval of Our Brothers, We have decreed that he be enrolled in the catalogue of saints worthy of veneration. We decree that his birth be celebrated worthily and solemnly by the universal Church on the fourth of October, the day on which he entered the kingdom of Heaven, freed from the prison of the flesh."[262]

May 25, AD 1230

After the canonization, Pope Gregory IX lays the cornerstone for the construction of the basilica in honor of St. Francis. It was completed two years later, and St. Francis's remains were translated.

This Pope, who had loved Francis exceedingly while he was still alive, not only honored him wondrously by inscribing him in the choir of the Saints, he also had a church erected in his glory, laying the first stone himself and then enriching it with sacred gifts and most precious ornaments. Two years after the canonization, the body of Saint Francis was removed from the place where it had previously been buried [the church of San Giorgio] and was solemnly translated to this new church. [263]

---

262 Gregory IX, Bull *Mira circa nos.*

263 *Legend of the Three Companions*, 1486.

Epilogue

Celano concludes his Life.

Behold, blessed father [Francis], we have attempted in our simplicity to praise, as best we could, your wondrous actions and to set forth to your glory at least some aspects of the innumerable virtues of your holiness. We are convinced that our words have taken away much of the splendor of your greatness because they are not able to express the wonders of so much perfection. We ask you and the readers to measure our affection by the commitment we have undertaken, happy that the human pen is surpassed by the height of such a wondrous life. For who, indeed, O great Saint, could feel in himself or impress upon others the ardor of your spirit? Who could give life to the ineffable impulses of love that continually rose from you to God? But we have written these pages, attracted by the sweet memory that we have of you, in the desire to pass it on, as long as we live, even if only stammering, to others.[264]

Bonaventure concludes his Legend.

We conclude this work with a sort of brief recap. Whoever has read the preceding pages to the end, let him reflect on this concluding consideration: the conversion that took place in a wondrous way, the efficacy in proclaiming the Word of God, the privilege of sublime virtues, the spirit of prophecy combined with the penetration of the Scriptures, the obedience on the part of creatures devoid of reason, the impression of the sacred stigmata, and the well-known Transitus from this world to Heaven are, in Francis, seven luminous testimonies that demonstrate and guarantee to the entire world that he, a distinguished herald of Christ, bears within himself the seal of the living God and, therefore, is worthy of veneration for the mission received, proposes to us an authentic doctrine, and is wondrous in sanctity.[265]

And now I ask you, beloved brothers, to meditate lovingly on the deeds of our fathers and brothers, to

264 Celano, *Second Life*, 817.
265 Bonaventure, *Minor Legend*, 1393.

try to understand them, and to strive to translate them into works of life in order to merit to be participants with them in the heavenly glory—to which may our Lord Jesus Christ lead us.[266]

---

266 *Anonymous of Perugia*, 1544.

Part V: *Miscellanea*

AD 1216

Pope Honorius III grants Francis's request for a plenary indulgence to all who visit the Portiuncula on August 2.

While blessed Francis was at St. Mary of the Portiuncula, the Lord revealed to him during the night that he should go to the Supreme Pontiff, Lord Honorius, who was temporarily residing in Perugia, to request an indulgence for the said church of St. Mary of the Portiuncula, which he had restored. Arising in the morning, he called Brother Masseo of Marignano, the companion with whom he was, and presented himself before Lord Honorius.

"Holy Father, I have just finished restoring for you a church in honor of the Virgin Mother of Christ. I beg your holiness to enrich it with an indulgence without offerings of money."

The Pope replied, "It is not appropriate to do so because whoever requests an indulgence must merit it by extending his hand to help. But nevertheless, tell me how many years you want me to set regarding the indulgence."

Saint Francis replied, "Holy Father, may your holiness grant not years but souls."

The Lord Pope continued, "In what way do you want souls?"

Blessed Francis declared, "Holy Father, if it pleases your holiness, I wish for all who come to this church, having confessed, repented, and been absolved by the priest, to be freed from punishment and guilt in Heaven and on earth from the day of their baptism until the day and hour of their entry into the aforementioned church."

The Lord Pope replied, "What you ask for is much, Francis. It is not customary for the Roman Curia to grant such an indulgence."

Then blessed Francis replied, "Lord, I do not ask this on my part but on the part of Him Who sent me, the Lord Jesus Christ."

Then, without hesitation, the Lord Pope burst out saying three times, "I am pleased that you have this indulgence."

However, those cardinals present replied, "Beware, Lord, that if you give such an indulgence there, you will destroy the one overseas [that is, the Holy Land], and the indulgence of the apostles Peter and Paul [that is, Rome] will be destroyed and reduced to nothing."

But the Lord Pope replied, "We have given it, and it is granted. We cannot [revoke it], and it is not appropriate to destroy what has been done. But We will modify it so that it is limited to one day only."

Then he called Saint Francis and said to him, "Behold, from now on, We grant that everyone who comes to and enters the aforementioned church, having confessed well and contritely, will be absolved from punishment and guilt. And We wish this to be valid every year for one day only [that is, on August 2], from First Vespers, including the night, until Vespers of the following day."

Blessed Francis, bowing his head, was leaving the palace, but the Lord Pope, seeing him leave, called him back and said to him, "O simple man, where are you going? What document do you carry away regarding this indulgence?"

But Francis replied, "Your word is enough for me. If it is the work of God, God Himself must manifest His work. I do not want any other document [related] to it. Instead, the paper must be the Blessed Virgin Mary, the notary must be Jesus Christ, and the angels must be the witnesses."[267]

---

267 *Diploma of Theobald*, 2706–2707.

Why the "whole world" is running after Francis

Saint Francis was once living in the place of the Portiuncula with Brother Masseo of Marignano, who was a man of great sanctity, discretion, and grace in speaking of God. For this reason, Saint Francis loved him greatly. One day, Saint Francis was returning from the forest where he had been praying. After he came out of the wood, Brother Masseo wanted to test how humble he was. So, he went to meet him and almost as a proverb said, "Why you, why you, why you?"

Saint Francis answered, "What is it that you mean?"

Brother Masseo said, "I say, why does the whole world follow you and every person seem to desire to see you, hear you, and obey you? You are not a handsome man, you do not possess great knowledge, and you are not noble. Then why does the whole world follow you?"

Upon hearing this, Saint Francis rejoiced in spirit, raised his face to Heaven, and remained for a long time with his mind raised to God. Returning to himself, he knelt down and gave praise and thanks to God.

Then, with great fervor of spirit, he turned to Brother Masseo and said, "Do you want to know why me? Do you want to know why me? Do you want to know why the whole world follows me? This I have [seen] from those eyes of the Most High God, which everywhere contemplate the good and the wicked: because His most holy eyes have not seen among sinners anyone more vile, more insufficient, or a greater sinner than me. Therefore, to perform that marvelous work that He intends to do, He has not found a more vile creature on earth, and therefore He has chosen me to confound the nobility, the greatness, the strength, the beauty, and the wisdom of the world, so that it may be known that every virtue and every good come from Him and not from the creature, and no person can boast in His sight. But he who boasts, let him boast in the Lord, to whom is all honor and glory for eternity."

Brother Masseo was so struck by such a humble answer, spoken with fervor, that he knew certainly that Saint Francis was truly rooted in humility.[268]

The importance of the Tau to St. Francis.

Among all other letters, the letter Tau was most familiar to him, and with it alone he signed notes and decorated the walls of his cells. In fact, the man of God, Brother Pacifico, the contemplator of celestial visions,

268 *The Little Flowers*, 1838.

with the eyes of the flesh saw on the blessed father's forehead a large Tau, which shone with golden splendor. From rational conviction and from Catholic faith, it seems right that he who was so taken with admirable love of the cross also became admirable because of the cross. Therefore, nothing is more truly suited to him than what is preached about the stigmata of the cross.[269]

Francis spent many months every year praying in hermitages. He even wrote a Rule for the friars, describing how Franciscan hermits should live.
(The Rule of Life in Hermitages)

Those who want to remain in hermitages to lead a religious life should be three brothers, or four at most; of these, let two be "mothers" and have two "sons," or one at least. The two that are "mothers" should maintain the life of Martha and the two "sons" the life of Mary, and have a single enclosure, in which each may have his cell to pray and sleep in.

And they are always to say Compline of the day immediately after sunset. And they should make sure to keep the silence. And they are to recite their Hours.

---

269 Celano, *Treatise of Miracles*, 828.

And they are to get up for Matins. And let the first thing they seek be the kingdom of God and his justice. And let them say Prime at the appropriate hour and, after Terce, conclude the silence so that they can speak and go to their "mothers," from whom, when they want to, they can beg alms, like little paupers, for love of the Lord God. And afterwards, they are to recite Sext and None and, at the appropriate hour, Vespers.

And as to the enclosure where they stay, they may not allow any person either to enter or to eat there.

Those brothers who are the "mothers" are to make sure they keep their distance from people and, on account of the obedience due their minister, shield their "sons" from people, so that nobody can get to speak with them. And those "sons" are not to speak with any person other than their "mothers" and their minister and custodian, when he wishes to visit them with the blessing of the Lord God.

The "sons," nonetheless, should now and then take over the duty of the "mothers," according to what arrangement they have come to about taking turns at intervals. As for everything above-mentioned, let them earnestly and carefully endeavor to observe it.[270]

---

270 St. Francis, *The Rule of Life in the Hermitages*, 136–138.

Francis exhorts the friars to live always as pilgrims.

He did not want the friars to live in any place, no matter how small, unless its owner was certain. In fact, he always required his sons to be pilgrims, that is, that they gather under someone else's roof, pass from one place to another peacefully, and feel nostalgia for their [heavenly] homeland.[271]

Francis exhorted the brothers to be especially devoted to the Eucharist.

Look to your dignity, brother priests, and be holy because He is holy. And as the Lord God has honored you above all men by entrusting you with this ministry, so you too should love Him more than all, reverence Him, and honor Him. It is a great wretchedness and a miserable weakness, in that having Him so present, you are concerned with something else in the entire world. May all humanity fear, may the entire universe tremble, and may the Heavens rejoice when, on the altar, in the hand of the priest, Christ, the Son of the living God, is present.

---

271 Celano, *Second Life*, 645.

O wondrous loftiness and stupendous dignity! O sublime humility! O humble sublimity! The Lord of the universe, God and Son of God, humbles Himself to such an extent as to hide Himself, for our salvation, under the meager appearance of bread! Behold, brethren, the humility of God, and pour out your hearts before Him; humble yourselves also, that you may be exalted by Him.

Therefore, hold nothing back for yourselves, so that He Who offers Himself totally to you may receive you totally.[272]

Wherefore, all those who saw the Lord Jesus according to humanity and did not see and believe according to the spirit and the divinity that He is the true Son of God were condemned. So also now all those who behold the Sacrament, which is sanctified by the words of the Lord upon the altar at the hand of the priest in the form of bread and wine, and do not see and believe according to the Spirit and Divinity that it is truly the Most Holy Body and Blood of our Lord Jesus Christ, are condemned. This is attested by the Most High Himself, Who says, "This is My body and the blood of My New Testament" (see Mk 14:22, 24; 1 Cor 11:24–25, translated from the original text), and, "He who eats

---

272 St. Francis, *Letter to the Entire Order*, 220–221.

of My Body and drinks of My Blood will have everlasting life" (see Jn 6:54, translated from the original text). Wherefore the Spirit of the Lord, Who dwells in His faithful ones, it is He Who is received in the Most Holy Body and Blood of the Lord. All others who do not share in that Spirit and presume to receive Him eat and drink judgment on themselves. [. . .] Behold: daily He humbles Himself as when from Heaven's royal throne He came down into the womb of the Virgin. Daily He Himself comes to us with like humility; daily He descends from the bosom of the Father upon the altar in the hands of the priest. And as He appeared to the Apostles in true flesh, so now He also shows Himself to us in the sacred bread. And as they, by their bodily sight, saw only His flesh, yet contemplating Him with the eyes of the spirit, believed Him to be very much God, so we also, as we see the bread and wine with our bodily eyes, are to see and firmly believe that it is His Most Holy Body and Blood, living and true. And in this way the Lord is always with His faithful, as He Himself says, "Behold, I am with you until the end of the world" (see Mt 28:20, translated from the original text).[273]

---

273 St. Francis, *First Admonition*, 144–145.

A Salutation to Our Lady.

Hail, O Lady, holy Queen,
holy Mother of God, Mary,
who are the virgin made Church,
and chosen by the Most Holy heavenly Father,
who has consecrated you
together with his Most Holy beloved Son
and with the Holy Spirit Paraclete;
you in whom there was and there is
every fullness of grace and every good.
Hail, his palace!
Hail, his tabernacle!
Hail, his abode!
Hail, his clothing!
Hail, his handmaid!
Hail, his Mother!
And hail you all, holy virtues,
who by the grace and illumination of the Holy Spirit
are infused into the hearts of the faithful,
so that from infidels
you make them faithful to God.[274]

274 St. Francis, *A Salutation of the Blessed Virgin Mary*, 259–260.

Francis and spiritual joy.

Francis's highest and most passionate commitment was to possess and preserve spiritual joy within himself. He said, "If the servant of God takes care to have and habitually maintain interior and exterior joy, joy that flows from a pure heart, the demons can do him no harm, for they will say, 'Since this servant of God remains joyful in tribulation as in prosperity, let us not find a way to enter him and do him harm.'"[275]

St. Francis explains "Perfect Joy" to Brother Leo.

One day, blessed Francis was at St. Mary [of the Angels] when he called Brother Leo and said, "Brother Leo, write [the following]."

He replied, "Behold, I am ready."

"Write," he said, "what true joy is: if a messenger comes and says that all the masters of Paris have entered the Order, write that this is not true joy. Likewise, if all the prelates from beyond the Alps, archbishops and bishops, and also the king of France and the king of England have entered [the Order], write that this is not true joy. Moreover, [if it is announced] that

275 *Legend of Perugia/Assisi Compilation*, 1653.

my brothers have gone among the infidels and have converted them all to the Faith, and furthermore that I have received from God such grace that the sick are healed and I perform many miracles, I tell you that in all these things there is no true joy."

"What then is true joy?" asked Brother Leo.

"If I return from Perugia in the dead of night and arrive here, and the winter weather is muddy and so cold that at the end of my habit there are icicles of frozen water that continually hit my legs, and blood comes from those wounds; and I, all muddy, cold, and icy, reach the door, and after I have knocked and called out for a long time, a friar comes and asks, 'Who is it?' and I answer, 'Brother Francis'; and he says, 'Go away; this is not a suitable time [for beggars] to go around, so you will not come in'; and since I insist, another answers, 'Go away! You are a simpleton and an idiot, and you cannot come here now. We are so many and such that we do not need you'; but still I remain before the door and say, 'For the love of God, welcome me this night'; and he answers, 'I will not do it. Go to the place of the Crucifers and ask there': then I tell you that if I have been patient and have not become anxious, in this is true joy, true virtue, and the salvation of the soul."[276]

St. Francis exorcises demons out of the city of Arezzo.

When they arrived near Arezzo, the city was entirely in turmoil and civil war, day and night, due to two factions that had long hated each other. Upon seeing this and hearing the unleashing of noises and screams day and night while he was staying in a hospital in the village outside the city, Francis saw a cloud of demons who were enjoying that uproar and inciting all the inhabitants to destroy their city with fire and other furies. Moved with compassion, he turned to Brother Silvester, who was a priest, a man of great faith, wondrous simplicity, and purity, and whom he venerated as a saint, and said to him, "Go before the gate of the city and in a loud voice command all the demons to leave."

Silvester rose and went before the gate of the city, where he commanded in a loud voice, "Praised and blessed be the Lord Jesus Christ! On behalf of Almighty God and by virtue of the holy obedience of Francis, I command all demons to leave this city!"

---

276 St. Francis, *On True and Perfect Joy*, 278.

Then, by the divine mercy and prayer of Francis, the inhabitants of Arezzo returned shortly thereafter to peace and harmony, and there was no need for any preaching.[277]

St. Francis tames a wolf in Gubbio.

Whilst Saint Francis was staying in the city of Gubbio, there appeared a very large, terrible, and ferocious wolf, who not only devoured animals but also men, such that all the citizens were in great fear because it often approached the city. As such, they all went armed when they left the city, as if they were going to war. But despite all this, they could not defend themselves from it whenever someone encountered it alone. Due to fear of this wolf, the townspeople came to such a point that no one dared leave the city.

Wherefore, having compassion for the men of the territory, Saint Francis wished to go out to meet this wolf, although the citizens did not advise him to do so at all. All the same, he made the sign of the most holy cross and went out of the city with his companions, placing all his trust in God. Those who accompanied him were afraid to go any farther, and Saint Francis

---

277 *Legend of Perugia/Assisi Compilation*, 1637.

took the road towards the place where the wolf was known to be, while many people followed at a distance and witnessed the miracle. Seeing such a multitude, the wolf ran towards St Francis with its mouth wide open.

When it approached him, Saint Francis made the sign of the most holy cross and cried out, "Come here, Brother Wolf! I command you in the name of Christ not to harm me or anyone else!" A wondrous thing to tell—immediately after Saint Francis made the sign of the cross, the terrible wolf closed its mouth and stopped running. Having obeyed the command, it came meekly as a lamb and threw itself at the feet of Saint Francis to lie down.

Saint Francis spoke to him thus, "Brother Wolf, you are doing much harm in these parts and have committed great evils, destroying and killing the creatures of God without [His] permission. Not only have you killed and devoured beasts, you have dared to kill men made in the image of God, for which you are worthy of the gallows as a thief and a most evil murderer. For this, all the people cry out and murmur against you, and this entire land is your enemy. But I, Brother Wolf, wish to make peace between you and them so that you will no longer offend them, and they will forgive you for every past offense, and neither men nor dogs will persecute you anymore."

Having said these words, the wolf moved its body, tail, and ears, and by bowing his head, showed that it accepted what Saint Francis said and that it wanted to observe it.

Saint Francis then said, "Brother Wolf, since you are pleased to make and keep this peace, I promise you that as long as you live, I will have your food provided for continually by the men of this land so that you will never suffer hunger again. For I know well that it is because of hunger that you have done every evil. But since I am obtaining this favor for you, Brother Wolf, I want you to promise me that you will never harm any human being or animal. Will you promise me this?" The wolf bowed its head, in a clear sign that it promised.

[. . .]

The said wolf lived two years in Gubbio and entered familiarly from door to door and house to house, without harming anyone and without any harm being done to it. It was fed courteously by the people, and as it went through the land and the houses, no dog ever barked at him. Finally, after two years, Brother Wolf died of old age. The citizens mourned this greatly, because seeing him go so meekly through the city, they became more convinced of the virtue and sanctity of Saint Francis.[278]

St. Francis and St. Clare share a meal in St. Mary of the Angels.

When Saint Francis was at Assisi, he often visited Saint Clare, giving her holy teachings. She had a great desire to eat with him once. [. . .] When the appointed day came, Saint Clare left the monastery with a companion, accompanied by the companions of Saint Francis, and came to Saint Mary of the Angels. And having devoutly greeted the Virgin Mary before her altar, where she had been tonsured and veiled, they led her around the place until it was time for dinner. In the meantime, Saint Francis had the table prepared on the level ground, as was his custom. And when the hour for dinner had come, Saint Francis and Saint Clare sat down together, followed by one of the companions of Saint Francis and the companion of Saint Clare, and then all the other companions humbly sat down at the table. At the first course, Saint Francis began to speak of God so sweetly, so loftily, so marvelously that, the

278 *The Little Flowers*, 1852.

abundance of divine grace descending upon them, they were all raptured in God.

While they were thus rapt with their eyes and hands raised to Heaven, the men of Assisi and Bettona and those of the surrounding countryside saw that Our Lady of the Angels and all the place and the forest that was then next to the place were burning strongly, and it seemed as if there was a great fire that consumed the church, the place, and the forest together. For this reason, the people of Assisi ran down there with great haste to put out the fire, truly believing that everything was burning. But arriving at the place and finding nothing burning, they entered inside and found Saint Francis with Saint Clare and all their companions rapt in God in contemplation and sitting around that humble table. From this, they certainly understood that it had been divine and not material fire that God had miraculously made appear to demonstrate and signify the fire of divine love with which the souls of these holy friars and nuns burned, from which they departed with great consolation in their hearts and with holy edification.

After a long time, Saint Francis and Saint Clare, together with the others, returning to themselves and feeling well-comforted by the spiritual food, cared little about the bodily food. And so, having finished that blessed dinner, Saint Clare, well-accompanied, returned to San Damiano.[279]

St. Francis composes a melody for St. Clare to console the sisters.

After Francis composed the *Canticle of the Creatures*, he also composed some holy words with a melody for the consolation and edification of the Poor Ladies, knowing how much they suffered because of his infirmity. Since he could not visit them in person, he sent them the words through his companions. In that canticle, he wanted to manifest to them his will, that is, that they should always live and behave humbly and be in accordance in fraternal love. He saw in fact that their holy life was not only a reason of fervor for the Order of the friars but was a source of edification for the entire Church. Knowing that, from the beginning of their conversion, they had led a harsh and poor existence, he was always moved by mercy and compassion towards them. In that canticle, therefore, he prayed that, as the Lord had gathered them together from

279 *The Little Flowers*, 1844.

many places to live in holy charity, poverty, and obedience, they should always live and die in these virtues.[280]

Francis and prayer.

His greatest charge was to keep himself away from earthly cares, so that not even for an instant, by contact with the dust of the world, was the serenity of his soul disturbed. He made himself insensitive to all external clamor, and guarding his external senses with all his efforts and controlling every movement of the soul, he lived absorbed in the Lord alone. As it is said of the bride in the Song of Songs, "My dove [made her dwelling] in the clefts of the rock, in the secret recesses of the cliff" (Sg 2:14). Truly, with joyful devotion, he wandered among the heavenly dwellings, and in complete annihilation of himself, he dwelt for a long time as if hidden in the wounds of the Savior. Therefore, he often sought solitary places to be able to turn his soul completely to God. However, when he deemed it appropriate, he did not hesitate for a moment to move into action to willingly dedicate himself to the salvation of others.

280 *Mirror of Perfection*, 1788.

His safe harbor was prayer, not for a few minutes, or empty, or pretentious but prolonged for a long time—full of devotion and serene humility. If he began [praying] in the evening, he barely finished by morning.

He was always intent on prayer, whether he was walking, sitting, or eating and drinking. At night, he went, alone, to abandoned and remote churches to pray. In this way, with the grace of the Lord, he managed to triumph over many fears and much spiritual anguish.[281]

Preaching through example.

Francis used to say, "The preacher must first draw from the secret of prayer what he will then pour out in his sermons. He must first warm himself internally, so as not to utter cold words externally."[282]

Let no friar preach against the form and ordinances of the Holy Church and [let him not preach] without having received permission from his minister. And let the minister be careful not to grant [the faculty to preach] to anyone without discretion. All the friars, however, should preach by their deeds.[283]

---

281 Celano, *First Life*, 444–445.

282 Celano, *Second Life*, 747–748.

283 St. Francis, *Earlier Rule*, 46.

This is the privilege that I want from the Lord for myself: never to have any privilege from anyone, except to show respect to all and, in obedience to the Holy Rule, to convert men more by example than by words.[284]

[Francis] was truly persevering, and he concerned himself with nothing but the things of the Lord. In fact, even when he preached the word of the Lord before thousands of people, he was calm and confident, as if he were speaking to a family friend. In his eyes, a huge crowd of people was like a single man, and with the same diligence that he used for the multitudes, he preached to a single person. From the purity of his heart, he drew the confidence of his discourse, and even without preparation, he would say wondrous things that had never been heard before.[285]

From the Writings of St. Francis:

"I, Brother Francis, the least of your servants, pray and beseech you, in the charity that is God, and with the desire to kiss your feet, that you humbly and lovingly accept and put into practice and observe these and the other words of our Lord Jesus Christ. [. . .] And

284 *Mirror of Perfection*, 1738.
285 Celano, *First Life*, 447.

all those who benevolently accept them, understand them, and send copies to others, if they persevere in them until the end, may the Father and the Son and the Holy Spirit bless them. Amen."[286]

"All who love the Lord with all their heart, with all their soul and mind, and with all their strength; love their neighbors as themselves; hate their bodies with their vices and sins; receive the body and blood of our Lord Jesus Christ; and produce fruits worthy of penance: oh, how blessed are those men and women when they do such things and persevere in them, because the Spirit of the Lord will rest upon them and will make his dwelling and dwell among them."[287]

"[Christ], who was rich above all else, wanted to choose poverty in this world, together with the most blessed Virgin, his mother."[288]

"And this was the will of his Father, that his blessed and glorious Son, whom he gave to us and was born for us, should offer himself as a sacrifice and victim through his own blood on the altar of the cross, not for himself, for through him all things were made, but as a

---

286 St. Francis, *Letter to the Faithful* 2, 206.

287 St. Francis, *Letter to the Faithful* 1, 178.

288 St. Francis, *Letter to the Faithful* 2, 181–182.

propitiation for our sins, leaving us an example that we should follow in his footsteps."[289]

"I see nothing corporeally of the Most High Son of God in this world except His Most Holy Body and Blood, which priests receive and which priests alone administer to others."[290]

"With all that is in me and more, I beg you that, when it seems fitting and expedient to you, [you should] humbly beseech the clergy to venerate above all else the Most Holy Body and Blood of our Lord Jesus Christ and His holy names and the written words that consecrate His Body. The chalices, corporals, altar ornaments, and everything else that serves for the sacrifice [of the Mass] should be of precious material. If the Most Holy Body of the Lord is poorly reposed in any place, according to the command of the Church, it should be placed and safeguarded by them in a precious place, and it should be carried with great veneration and administered to others with discretion. Also, the names and written words of the Lord, wherever they are found in unclean places, should be collected and should be placed in a suitable place."[291]

---

289 St. Francis, *Letter to the Faithful* 2, 184.

290 St. Francis, *Testament*, 113.

291 St. Francis, *First Letter to the Custodians*, 242–243.

"Know that in the sight of God there are some very high and sublime realities that at times among men are considered vile and despicable; other [realities], on the other hand, are [considered] precious and admired among men, though before God they are considered very vile and despicable."[292]

"We must never desire to be above others; rather, we must be servants and subjects to every human creature for the love of God."[293]

"To Brother Anthony [of Padua], my bishop, Brother Francis sends greetings. I am pleased that you teach sacred theology to the brothers, provided that, as is written in the Rule, in this occupation you do not extinguish the spirit of prayer and devotion."[294]

"Brother Leo, your brother Francis sends you greetings and peace. My son, I say to you, as a mother, that everything that we said while on the road, I summarize briefly in this word of counsel, and there is no need for you to come to me to counsel you, because this is what I advise you: In whatever way you think best to please the Lord God and to follow in his footsteps and his poverty, do it with the blessing of the Lord God

292 St. Francis, *Second Letter to the Custodians*, 246.

293 St. Francis, *Letter to the Faithful* 2, 199.

294 St. Francis, *Letter to Brother Anthony*, 251.

and with my obedience. And if it is necessary for you, so that you may have other consolation, that your soul return to me, and you want it, come!"[295]

Francis wrote twenty-eight Admonitions. More than "warnings," they were brief, practical applications of Scripture or other spiritual teachings.

"The one who eats from the tree of the knowledge of good is he who appropriates his will [to himself] and exalts himself for the good things that the Lord says and works in him."[296]

"Those who are placed above others should boast of that higher office as much as if they were appointed to the office of washing the feet of their brothers."[297]

"Indeed, one truly loves his enemy who does not grieve over the injury that [the other] does to him but, driven by the love of God, burns because of the sin in [the other's] soul."[298]

"The servant of God does not know how much patience and humility he has in himself as long as he

---

295 St. Francis, *Letter to Brother Leo*, 249–250.

296 St. Francis, *Admonitions* 2, 147.

297 St. Francis, *Admonitions* 4, 152.

298 St. Francis, *Admonitions* 9, 158.

is being satisfied. But when the time comes that those who ought to satisfy him rise up against him, as much patience and humility as he has in this matter, so much will he have and no more."[299]

"Those people are true peacemakers who, in all the things they endure in this world, for the love of our Lord Jesus Christ, maintain peace in soul and body."[300]

"The man sins who wants to receive more from his neighbor than he wants to give of himself to the Lord God."[301]

"Blessed is the servant who does not consider himself better when he is magnified and exalted by men than when he is considered vile, simple, and despicable. For what a man is before God, so much he is and no more."[302]

"Where there is charity and wisdom,
there is neither fear nor ignorance.
Where there is patience and humility, there
is neither anger nor disturbance.

299 St. Francis, *Admonitions* 13, 162.

300 St. Francis, *Admonitions* 15, 164.

301 St. Francis, *Admonitions* 17, 166.

302 St. Francis, *Admonitions* 19, 169.

Where there is poverty with joy, there
is neither greed nor avarice.
Where there is quiet and meditation, there
is neither worry nor dissipation.
Where there is the fear of the Lord to guard his
house, there the enemy cannot find a way in.
Where there is mercy and discretion, there
is neither superfluity nor harshness."[303]

"Blessed is the servant who stores up in the treasury of Heaven the good things that the Lord shows him and does not desire to reveal them to men for a reward, since the Most High Himself will reveal His works to whomever He pleases. Blessed is the servant who keeps the secrets of the Lord in his heart."[304]

303 St. Francis, *Admonitions* 27, 177.

304 St. Francis, *Admonitions* 28, 178.

The Blessing of St. Francis

The Lord bless you and keep you.
May he show you his face
and have mercy on you.
May he turn his face toward
you and give you peace.

Translator's Bio

Bret Thoman, OFS, was born and raised in the suburbs of Atlanta, Georgia (USA). Since 2014, he has lived in Loreto, Italy, with his wife and three children. He has been a member of the Secular Franciscan Order (Third Order of St. Francis) since 2003. He has a master's degree in Italian from Middlebury College, a BA from the University of Georgia in foreign languages, and a certificate in Franciscan Studies. Bret is an FAA-licensed pilot and has logged over 3,500 hours of flight time. Bret's main activity is organizing pilgrimages for St. Francis Pilgrimages, the company he founded in 2004. He leads individuals and groups through Italy, including to the Franciscan sites in Central Southern Italy.